How to Navigate Strategic Alliances and Joint Ventures

How to Navigate Strategic Alliances and Joint Ventures

A Concise Guide For Managers

Meeta Dasgupta

BEP BUSINESS EXPERT PRESS

How to Navigate Strategic Alliances and Joint Ventures: A Concise Guide For Managers

Cover image licensed by Ingram Image, StockPhotoSecrets.com

First published in 2020 by
Business Expert Press, LLC
222 East 46th Street, New York, NY 10017
www.businessexpertpress.com

ISBN-13: 978-1-95152-728-0 (paperback)
ISBN-13: 978-1-95152-729-7 (e-book)

Business Expert Press Strategic Management Collection

Collection ISSN: 2150-9611 (print)
Collection ISSN: 2150-9646 (electronic)

Cover and interior design by Exeter Premedia Services Private Ltd., Chennai, India

First edition: 2020

10 9 8 7 6 5 4 3 2 1

Printed in the United States of America.

To my family

Abstract

It is not only the smaller organizations, but also the larger organizations like IBM, GE, and Microsoft that are realizing the importance of collaborations and partnerships to achieve their business objectives. In contrast to a decision to go for an acquisition, a decision to go for a strategic alliance demands a collaborative mindset. Organizations in order to create independent and joint values are entering into strategic alliances with their suppliers, customers, and even their competitors. Every alliance, whether a contractual or an equity alliance or a joint venture, follows a lifecycle. A strategic alliance starts with having a clarity on the business case of the alliance, followed by selection of a partner, negotiating the terms and conditions of the alliance, managing an alliance, and finally, assessing the performance of an alliance. Decisions have to be taken by executives at each stage of the alliance lifecycle. Anticipated revenues and other sources of financial value remain unrealized if inadequate decisions are taken and alliances fail or underperform. This book takes a reader through the different stages of an alliance lifecycle and discusses and debates on the decisions to be taken. The book also demonstrates the various challenges faced by executives in an alliance. The author by sharing various practical incidents tries to connect the readers to the various decisions involved and taken by organizations during an alliance. This book is perfect for managerial executives who are contemplating proposing a strategic alliance for their organizations or are part of an organization juggling various ongoing alliances, alliance managers, and business development professionals. In short, the content of the book should be of interest to anyone for whom alliances are a topic of interest.

Keywords

strategic alliance; joint venture; business case for an alliance; partner selection; risk assessment; value creation; negotiating an alliance; alliance management; assessment of the alliance

Contents

Acknowledgments

First and foremost, I would like to thank the management executives and participants of various programs at the Management Development Institute, Gurgaon, who have interacted with me in classroom sessions and in various forums. These interactions have given me interesting insights on various decisions their organizations have taken when they decided to go for a strategic alliance. Effort has been made to share these insights and interesting anecdotes with the readers.

I would like to thank my family—my parents, my husband, and my children, who have been a constant source of inputs, support, and inspiration to me, and my brother who has patiently responded to a number of my queries on the subject. It is their support that gave me the motivation to initiate writing this book.

I would also like to thank my colleagues at the institute, who had written books with BEP and other publishing houses, for encouraging me to attempt writing this book. Their experience with writing books and account of their journey motivated me to endeavor the same.

I am grateful to the reviewers of the book for painstakingly providing comments and feedback to improve the content of the book.

Most important of all, I thank God for making me accomplish what I had started with.

CHAPTER 1

What Are Strategic Alliances?

Do You Expect to Conquer the World Independently?

Over the past number of years, both domestic and international strategic alliances have grown exponentially in number and are now a very popular instrument in the current competitive global environment. Many multinational organizations that had previously shunned alliances are becoming increasingly involved in partnerships. Organizations have realized the importance of strategic alliances as a means of complementing their generic competitive strategies. Organizations have realized that it is challenging to take on the world by oneself. They have realized that they can no longer develop all the resources, technologies, and products to compete in the current dynamic marketplace. Strategic alliances, becoming a critical part of the overall strategy of the organization, are being used to develop critical skills, knowledge, and capabilities that it lacks and to grow product and service offerings. The *make versus buy*[1] decision, which once confronted decision makers, has expanded and has become more complex—*make versus buy versus partner* decision. This argument is supported by a study conducted by Accenture, which reported that about 25 percent of the executives said alliances accounted for at least 15 percent of their market value.[2] A study conducted by KPMG professionals in 2017, wherein they surveyed around 50 alliance experts from around the world, supports the importance organizations give to strategic alliances in their

---

[1] Gardiner, S.C., and Jr. J.H. Blackstone. 1991. "The 'Theory of Constraints' and the Make-Or-Buy Decision." *International Journal of Purchasing and Materials Management* 27, no. 3, pp. 38–43.

[2] Palmer, D., and P. Mullaney. 2001. "Building Better Alliances." *Outlook*, pp. 53–57.

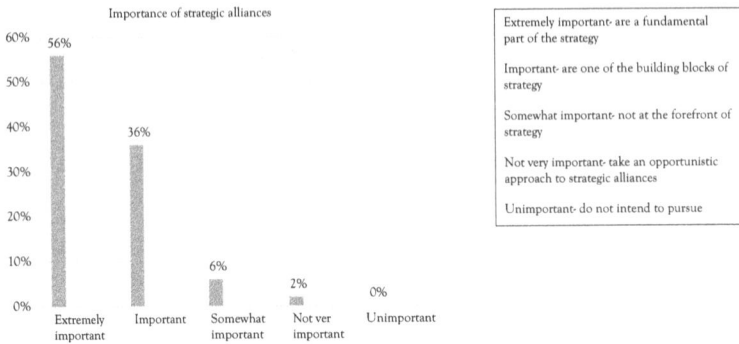

Figure 1.1 graphically exhibits the opinion

Figure 1.1 Importance of strategic alliances in overall corporate strategy

overall corporate strategy.[3] Figure 1.1 graphically exhibits the opinion voiced by the experts in the study.

IBM's entry into the personal computer industry was greatly facilitated by its willingness to rely on outsiders for development and production: Intel for chips, Microsoft for operating systems software, Epson for peripherals, and a number of Asian vendors for other components. General Motors partners include Isuzo, Suzuki, and Toyota. While taking the example of Tata Motors, some 100 component makers worked with the organization for over three years to create Nano. Ratan Tata was able to keep his promise and deliver a car for INR 100,000, the Nano with help from them, most of them homespun Indian outfits. This exemplifies the fact that organizations, big and small, are accepting the importance of alliances to compete and win at the global level. It is clear that strategic alliances as an organizational structure for global organizations have become very popular.

A very big contributor toward this partnership drive has been the emergence of global integration. Global integration can be looked through the lens of globalization of demand, globalization of supply, globalization of competition, and globalization of strategy. Demand from customers is not restricted to a particular geography. Their tastes have become global,

---

[3] Global Strategy Group. "Strategic Alliances: A Real Alternative to M&A?" https://assets.kpmg/content/dam/kpmg/ie/pdf/2018/01/ie-strategic-alliances-a-real-alternative-to-ma.pdf

their preferences becoming standardized, thereby leading to the evolution of a global marketplace. The concept of supply globalization works in tandem to the House of Innovation proposed by C.K. Prahalad in his book *New Age of Innovation*, wherein an organization, in order to satisfy one customer, needs to have access to unlimited resources. Companies also, in their drive toward cost efficiency, have diversified their supply chain management activities across the globe. This makes it imperative for them to tie up with the local players of different geographies. Apple's iPhone has its various parts manufactured by suppliers in China, Japan, and Taiwan.[4] Competition has become global. Gone are the days when organizations would compete with local players. It is a global battlefield with global corporate stalwarts pitted against each other. Tata Motors is not only competing against the likes of Maruti Suzuki and Mahindra and Mahindra, but due to acquisition of Jaguar Land Rover also with luxury carmakers. The strategic choices that organizations have to make or the decisions they have to take also have taken a global perspective. A change in the business scenario anywhere in the world might impact an organization's decisions.

Changing Dynamics of the World

Not only has the importance of strategic alliances picked up, but the dynamics have also changed. *Triadization* or strategic alliances among the *triad* regions of North America, Western Europe, and Japan has given way to alliances with the big emerging market countries of India, China, Brazil, Indonesia, and others. Examples are as follows:

- Walmart making an inroad into the Indian retail industry by entering into a joint venture with Bharti Enterprises.
- Fiat entering into a strategic alliance with Tata Motors for joint production of cars and distribution of Fiat cars.

---

[4] Gould, S. and A. Antonio Villas-Boas. 2016. "Here's Where All the Components of Your iPhone Come From." April 13, 2016, https://businessinsider.in/Hereswhere-all-the-components-of-your-iPhone-come-from/articleshow/51802648.cms

- Cafe Coffee Day tying up with Swiggy, an online food delivery startup, to deliver coffee and snacking items at the doorstep.
- Spotify getting into an alliance with Uber to provide stereo control and personalized experience to Uber riders.

Multinationals, realizing the importance of the emerging markets, have changed their focus to entering into collaborations with Indian companies.

Need for an Organization to Enter Into a Strategic Alliance

Executives of every organization planning to grow and achieve certain strategic outcomes are posed with this question sooner or later during their lifespan.

The decisions can be shown across a continuum, as illustrated in Figure 1.2.

An organization has a choice; to achieve its objectives independently, also referred to as organic growth, to go and acquire another organization, or enter into collaboration with another; the latter two choices also referred to as inorganic growth. In the first case, the organization should have the resources and capabilities that would help it to achieve its objectives independently. In case the organization lacks the resources and capabilities to develop those resources independently, it can go and acquire another organization that has all the resources and capabilities the organization lacks. But, the organization should be prepared to own the

How does my organization achieve its objectives?

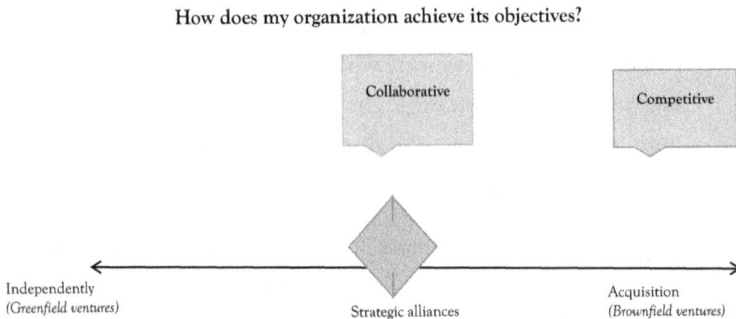

Collaborative

Competitive

Independently
(Greenfield ventures)

Strategic alliances

Acquisition
(Brownfield ventures)

Figure 1.2 Choices for an organization

complete risks and liabilities of the acquired organization. In case that is not something that the organization is prepared for, it can consider entering into a collaboration. Decision of a strategic alliance lies somewhere in between on the continuum.

For successful implementation of a global strategy, it becomes essential that a multinational enterprise should carefully implement its entry strategy for each international market because the success or failure of investment in one market will critically influence the activities in the complete network.

According to the real options theory, strategic alliances confer valuable options to expand or grow under conditions of uncertainty. By entering into strategic alliances, organizations are able to limit their downside losses to an initial, limited commitment, as well as position itself to expand. Organizations can spur their growth or market entry strategies either through greenfield investments or through mergers and acquisitions. In capital and research-intensive industries, organizations can spread risk over multiple capital providers by engaging in international joint ventures, rather than outright acquisitions. By entering into international strategic alliances, multinational corporations (MNCs) can also rely upon local partners' resources to manage risk, including their local knowledge, relationships with local government, and so forth. International strategic alliances lead to higher value creation, particularly in the presence of asymmetric information between the partners.

Strategic alliances help to increase efficiency. Cooperation leads to increased output, lower prices, and creation of new or better products. Two underlying sources of efficiencies are reduced costs and increased investment incentives. Production and distribution costs are reduced by realizing potential scope and scale economies and by eliminating duplicative activities. Increased technological rivalry stimulates innovation. Research and development (R&D) activities when done in coordination would not only speed up the development of new products at lower cost, but also help to achieve scale economies through joint ownership of a single large production facility.

Many international strategic alliances in developing countries are driven with the aim to grow, with research showing that the growth potential in case of emerging economies' alliances was more than that of developed economies' alliances. Organizations in industries with high technology components such as electronics, computers, and chemicals tend to have greater growth option values than those in food processing or tire manufacturing industries. International strategic alliances provide access to foreign markets, which otherwise would have been difficult to access due to insufficient capital, technology, and personnel.

Although mergers and acquisitions provide more control on the operations of the combined entity, interestingly, mergers and acquisitions, rather than being a secret to financial success, can destroy shareholder value more than they can create it. Their approximate failure rate ranges anywhere from 50 to 90 percent, with more than 60 percent destroying shareholder value. When there is uncertainty and stakes are high, partnerships can be an attractive alternative to going alone or indulging in mergers and acquisitions.

The organization belongs to a slow cycle industry; does a strategic alliance add value to the organization?

The answer to this question leaves no doubt in one's mind when one talks of a fast cycle industry, like information technology, that is moving at a very fast pace. Technologies become redundant at a very fast pace. In such industries, a strategic alliance not only helps organizations to shorten the product development cycle time and speed up entry to market, but also helps to share the R&D expenditure and the associated risks. An organization in a slow cycle market can use a strategic alliance to gain access to restricted markets and to maintain market stability by establishing standards.

The market power theory says that an organization, in order to compete successfully, should strengthen its market position. Strategic alliances are also formed to alter the basis of competition. To remain competitive or eliminate competition, organizations may enter into strategic alliances, thereby strengthening their market position.

Understanding the Term Strategic Alliances

According to Webster's Dictionary, an alliance is an *association of interests*. In a broad context, the term *alliance* refers to "relationships that provide opportunities for mutual benefit and results beyond what any single organization or sector could realise alone" (Austin 2000; p. 47). In the context of business and management, alliance can be defined as any voluntarily initiated cooperative agreement between organizations that *involves exchange, sharing, or codevelopment*, and it can include contributions by partners of capital, technology, or organization-specific assets. "Compatibility of goals, synergy among partners, an appropriate value chain and partners who make approximately equal contributions in relevant areas are some of the key success factors for strategic alliances" (Dwyer et al. 2011). Complementarities of market and compatibility of resources drive the formation of alliances in firms and the rate of their performance and survival.

What makes alliances unique is that independent companies coordinate their actions and resources and also share risks and rewards. Alliances generally involve some degree of exclusivity. Though not always, but often, strategic alliances are perceived to be temporary vehicles for growth and attaining objectives.

For a strategic alliance, it is essential that:

- Two or more organizations unite to pursue a set of agreed-upon goals and remain independent subsequent to the formation of the alliance.
- Partner organizations share the benefits of the alliance and control over the performance of the assigned tasks.
- Partner organizations contribute on a continuing basis in one or more key strategic areas.

History is replete with examples of companies entering into strategic alliances. Timex getting into a strategic alliance with Titan for the distribution of its watches through the latter's vast distribution network. IBM got into an alliance with Wipro, wherein Wipro would market and integrate IBM's wide range of server and storage products to address customer needs in India and Asia Pacific region. Walmart got into an alliance with Bharti Enterprises to set up Best Price Modern Wholesale stores that offered best fixed and fair prices for a wide assortment and variety of high-quality merchandise. Hero Motors got into an alliance with Honda, Japan, to manufacture fuel-efficient low-cost motorcycles. At the global level, Starbucks got into an alliance with Barnes and Noble to provide coffee breaks to customers while they browse through the latest bestsellers shelf. Interestingly, the business model of international giants like McDonalds, Kentucky Fried Chicken, Hilton, Hyatt, and Pepsi is surviving on the basis of franchisee agreements entered into with players in various countries.

Is there a limit to the number of partners in an alliance?

Alliances are not restricted to two partners. Companies can enter into an alliance with a single partner organization or with multiple organizations to form an alliance network. For example, General Motors entered into an alliance with Toyota, Isuzo, Suzuki, and SAAB so that it could compete effectively with Ford Motors that was part of another alliance network with Nissan, Mazda, Kia, and Jaguar. For example, Star alliance had 28 member airlines, whereas Sky Team alliance is a network of 19 airlines.

The concept of one-to-one partnering has shifted toward managing a network of alliances. Companies feel that operating in networks helps them to hedge against future technological challenges. They always have the option, when working with multiple partners, to reposition themselves in adjacent knowledge networks.

Are strategic alliances restricted to corporates?

Alliances are not restricted to corporates or organizations. Nations also see the benefit of alliances. The concept of regional economic integration and formation of agreements between nations like the North American Free Trade Agreement (NAFTA), European Union (EU), Association of South East Asian Nations (ASEAN), and so on are steps in the direction. Member countries, through regional economic integration, make efforts to promote free and fair trade on a regional basis. Member countries continue to be in the alliance till they feel it is creating value for them more than they would be able to create when working independently. The formation of International Solar Alliance, an inter-government treaty-based organization, marks the coming together of like-minded countries and businesses that share United Kingdom's commitment to deliver clean, affordable energy, and thereby help to end poverty. These sources of energy are considered to be the lifeline for

| Mutual service consortium | Joint venture Licensing/Franchising arrangement | Value chain partnerships |

Weak and distant relationship among partners   *Strong and close relationship among partners*

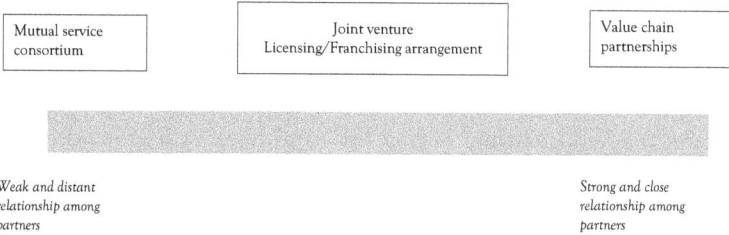

Figure 1.3 Continuum of strategic alliances

the rural community.[5] But, the focus of this book is alliances between corporates.

Types of Strategic Alliances

For the purpose of our understanding, and for the purpose of the book, the term *strategic alliance* has been taken in an inclusive manner. It relates with any alliance entered between two or more players for a mutually decided objective, to achieve mutually beneficial strategic outcomes, and ultimately to achieve competitive advantage.

Based on the proximity between the alliance partners and the strength of the relationship, strategic alliances can be represented along a continuum, as illustrated in Figure 1.3. Alliance partners might enter into a consortium wherein alliance partners have come together for a purpose, with no sharing of assets and revenues. A good example would be DIAL (Delhi International Airport Authority Limited), which is a consortium set up as a joint venture between GMR Group (54 percent), Airport Authority of India (26 percent), and Fraport AG and Emran Malaysia (10 percent each). The concession to manage, operate, and develop the Indira Gandhi International Airport was awarded to the consortium in 2006 for 30 years, extendable by another 30 years.[6]

What is the need to form a consortium?

---

[5] Aditi, K. April 17, 2018. "UK Joins International Solar Alliance to Mark Narendra Modi." https://livemint.com/Industry/J6uQDEC9pqS7ZqQzfm-mzuJ/UK-joins-International-Solar-Alliance-to-mark-Narendra-Modi.html (accessed October 08, 2018).

[6] Delhi International Airport (P) Ltd., http://gmrgroup.in/dial.aspx

In case of large complex projects, especially nuclear projects or other projects of the government, wherein varied specialized skills are required, which are rarely possessed by a single organization, organizations form a consortium. Organizations having the requisite skills join hands to bid for such projects. The structure of a consortium not only gives them the independence that is required to operate independently, but also helps them share the risk involved in such complex projects.

On the other end of the continuum are value chain partnerships where alliance partners need to coordinate closely and synchronize their working so as to create value. Value chain partnerships are long-term arrangements entered into by organizations either with their suppliers or with their distributors for mutual advantage. Any gap in the relationship or in the working of the partners will lead to lags in the value chain output. For example, Toyota's alliance with its various suppliers or Nike's alliance with its retail partners.

Other forms of strategic alliances are licensing agreements and joint ventures. In case of the former, the licensor licenses its technology to the licensee for production. In return, the licensee is entitled to pay royalty or license fee on the number of units produced using the licensed technology. A transaction very similar to licensing is franchising relationships in the services industry: McDonalds, KFC, Pizza Hut, Dominos, Bikanervala, and so on. Some of the most common nonequity alliances include cobranding, comarketing, strategic outsourcing, cooperative bidding, and joint purchasing. A joint venture leads to the creation of an independent legal entity by the alliance partners; allocating ownership, operational responsibilities, financial risks, and rewards to each member while maintaining their separate identity and autonomy. An important aspect that differentiates a joint venture from any other strategic alliance is the formation of a separate legal entity.

Is a cartel a form of strategic alliance?

Absolutely, a cartel survives on a mindset of cooperation among the participating organizations or countries. A very good example is the Organization for the Petroleum Exporting Countries (OPEC), an intergovernmental organization of 14 nations. The cartel's mission to "coordinate and unify the petroleum policies of its member countries and ensure the stabilization of oil markets, in order to secure an efficient, economic and regular supply of petroleum to consumers, a steady income to producers, and a fair return on capital for those investing in the petroleum industry"[7] has an influence on global oil prices. Although a cartel is a formal agreement among the participating organizations, in countries like India, a cartel is considered to be an illegal arrangement by the Competition Commission of India (CCI), the regulatory body that promotes free competition and free play of market forces in the country. Organizations following collusive practices that hamper the market forces come under the scanner of the CCI.

Thin Balance Between Cooperation and Competition

Alliances draw balance between cooperation and competition, thus posing a dilemma for management executives, as illustrated in Figure 1.4.

Alliances formed between manufacturers and their suppliers or their distributors present low potential of conflict between the partners. Alliances formed that are intra-industry and among noncompeting organizations require high level of interaction among partners. For example, an alliance between Renault and Nissan requires the partners to share their platforms to jointly develop model of cars that they independently sell. The partners at the time of the alliance do not regard each other as rivals, although, later on they have the potential to be competitors. Alliances formed between competitors require a high level of interaction among

Maintaining Flexibility
Protecting Core Competencies
Enhancing Learning
Maximizing Value

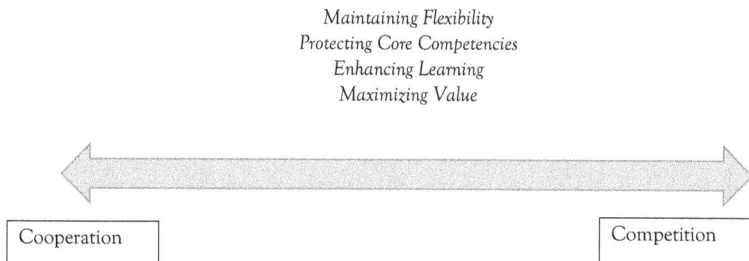

| Cooperation | | Competition |

Figure 1.4 Balance between cooperation and competition

---

[7] OPEC, from https://en.wikipedia.org/wiki/OPEC#cite_note-4 (accessed December 22, 2017)

partners to create value, with the partners competing directly in the final market. An apt example is the joint venture formed between Airtel, Vodafone, and Idea to share towers and bring in more efficiency of operations in the telecommunication industry. Each of these players, however, competes in the market for customers. Organizations from unrelated industries also come together to form alliances. For example, DuPont and Sony came together to form an alliance to develop optical memory storage products. Neither of the organizations possesses the technological or market know-how that is required to succeed alone. Through this alliance, they expect to develop a product that they will subsequently manufacture and market independently. The joint activity requires limited interaction between partners. However, being potential rivals in the memory storage market adds a dimension of conflict between the two partners.

Horizontal joint ventures that link competing organizations from the same industry are anti-competitive in nature because of the increased market power derived from horizontal linkages between the parent organizations. Nonhorizontal joint ventures that link together competing organizations from the same industry are more likely to increase competition as they provide entry into new markets.

Role of Foreign Direct Investment Regulations of a Country

Do the foreign direct investment regulations of a country influence the formation of a joint venture?

The foreign direct investment regulations of a country guide the formation of strategic alliances. Industries protected by the foreign direct investment (FDI) regulations of the country block the entry of foreign players. FDI rules allowing investment by foreign players up to a certain limit, say 26, 49, or 74 percent, restrict the maximum stake of the foreign player up to the specified limit. For example, in the aviation industry, when Jet entered into an equity alliance with Etihad, the government allowed foreign airlines to hold maximum of 49 percent in Indian carriers. Etihad took a 24 percent stake in Jet Airways. Similarly, in the insurance industry, when Sun Life Financials entered into an alliance with the Aditya Birla group, the maximum stake allowed to a foreign player was 26 percent. It is advisable that when designing a joint venture, one should look at the investment climate in the international market. A more favorable investment climate renders joint ventures less vulnerable to the downside effects of unanticipated government-induced uncertainties.

Benefits of an Alliance

There are various ways in which strategic alliances benefit organizations. The most common reasons being:

- *Enter new markets:* An organization that invests in a foreign country usually suffers from the *liability of foreignness,* a competitive disadvantage that arises from the inability of the organization to understand the foreign market and operate in them. An alliance might help organizations to enter new markets, either in terms of new products and services or new geographies. In emerging markets, where regulatory bodies have restrictions with respect to the FDI in particular indus-tries, a strategic alliance with a local player enables entry into those markets. Entry into new products and services is fraught with various risks. An alliance helps to share those risks. For example, in the Jet–Etihad alliance, wherein the government had put a restriction of 49 percent of the FDI, an alliance with Jet gave an opportunity to Etihad to enter into India.
- *Safeguard against uncertainties:* In dynamic market conditions, an alliance helps organizations to hedge and safeguard against various uncertainties. Alliances, in effect, give organizations an option to explore future growth and development. The organization invests in an alliance and has the option either to exit from the alliance or to get more deeply involved if the business holds promise. Drawing parallel with the financial world, an option is the right to buy or sell a security within a given period at a predetermined price. The option if not exercised within the given period expires. The key value of the option rests on the flexibility it offers to act in the future

as new events unfold. The greater the uncertainty of future events, the higher the value of the flexibility.

- *Get access to critical complementary assets:* For successful commercialization of a product or service, organizations need complementary assets, varying from downstream activities like marketing and distribution, after-sales service to upstream activities like procurement of raw materials and manufacturing. Strategic alliances enable organizations to get access to the complementary resources they lack. For example, in the Jet Etihad alliance Jet's domestic tie-ups and routes complemented Etihad's international routes.

- *Learn new capabilities and acquire new skillsets:* Strategic alliances enable organizations to learn new capabilities and acquire new skill sets, which otherwise would not have been possible if operating independently. Or, acquisition of those capabilities would have been a time-consuming and an expensive process. In fact, organizations in an alliance are in a race, and the organization that learns faster and attains its objectives would like to exit the alliance. These learning races tilt the bargaining power in favor of organizations that have managed to learn more than the other.

- For example, in the joint venture between General Motors and Toyota, the latter managed to learn the tricks of operating in the U.S. market faster than the former learning the art of executing lean manufacturing system in its various plants.

- *Reduce political risk:* The decision to enter into new markets is loaded with political risk, especially because of the high level of information asymmetry. Risk is also high because of the uncertainty in various government rules and regulations with respect to the operations of multinational enterprises in various industries. Strategic alliances help multinational enterprises, especially to ward off this risk. Their local counterpart is in a better position to understand and manage the political nuances.

- *Attain economies of scale:* Two organizations operating in the same industry by getting into an alliance can enjoy benefits of economies of scale and reduced average cost per unit. This can produce a potential barrier for entry of would-be competitors into the industry. It can also help organizations to compete more effectively with the existing set of competitors.

- *Strengthen competitive position:* Organizations can use strategic alliances to change the dynamics of the industry, establish new industry standards, and thereby strengthen their competitive position. For example, IBM by collaborating with a number of organizations like Samsung, ST Microelectronics, Freescale Semiconductor, and so on for R&D and manufacturing of semiconductors changed the dynamics of operating and competing in the semiconductor industry. Similarly, Tesla's portfolio of strategic alliances with leading companies in the automotive and other industries has spelt success for the organization. Tesla's alliance with Daimler Chrysler gave access to superior engineering expertise and funds, which saved the organization from potential bankruptcy. The alliance with Toyota enabled Tesla to buy NUMMI joint venture plants in United States and also learn large-scale high-quality manufacturing. The alliance with Panasonic, Japan, the consumer electronics organization and a world leader in battery technology provided a route to the two organizations to do joint manufacturing of the lithium-ion battery. The alliance with Starbucks helped Barnes and Noble to stay ahead of the curve.

Alliances, therefore, help companies to manage risk. They help them to share the costs of risky projects, hedge risks, reduce the cost of responding to unpredictable trends, and most important of all, explore future opportunities.

Emerging Market Alliances

Global companies are eying emerging markets for growth. On the other hand, companies in the emerging markets are looking for ways to be part of the expanding global economy. Alliances, therefore, serve as an obvious solution for both sides. Global companies usually contribute intangible

```
                    ┌─────────────────────────────────────────────┐
                    │ Sustained / Stable Balance of Power          │
                    │                                              │
                    │ (Successful for both Partners-May continue   │
                    │  for decades)                                │
                    └─────────────────────────────────────────────┘

                    ┌─────────────────────────────────────────────┐
                    │ Power Shifts towards Local Partner           │
                    │                                              │
                    │ (Local partner may acquire - may succeed     │
                    │  or fail)                                    │
  ┌──────────┐      └─────────────────────────────────────────────┘
  │ Initial  │
  │ Alliance │      ┌─────────────────────────────────────────────┐
  └──────────┘      │ Power Shifts towards Global Partner          │
                    │                                              │
                    │ (Global partner may acquire - may succeed    │
                    │  or fail)                                    │
                    └─────────────────────────────────────────────┘

                    ┌─────────────────────────────────────────────┐
                    │ Collision of Power                           │
                    │                                              │
                    │ (Alliance likely to be short - lived-neither │
                    │  partner gains)                              │
                    └─────────────────────────────────────────────┘
```

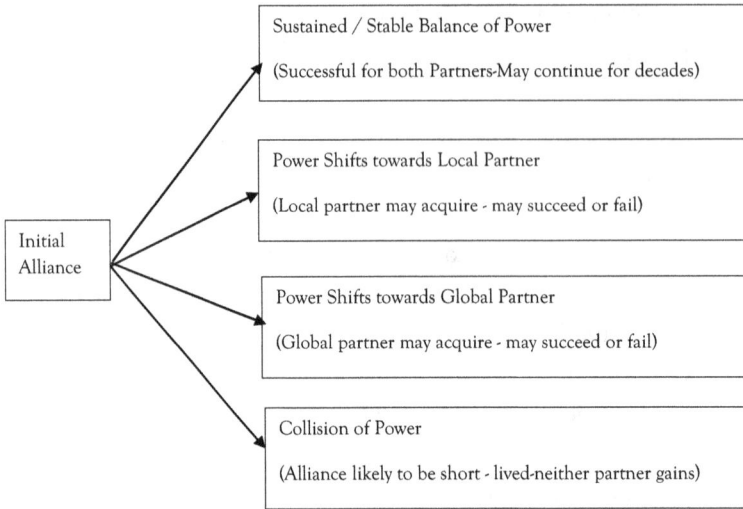

Figure 1.5 *Possible outcomes of alliances in emerging markets*

assets like technology, brand name, skills, and expertise. Local companies provide an insight into local customer behavior, knowledge about the market, a manufacturing base, and possibly a network with regulatory bodies.

Do all the alliances in emerging markets follow the same trajectory?

Possibly, no. As illustrated in Figure 1.5, history sees four different outcomes of strategic alliances in India.

We have examples of joint ventures like that of between Honda and Hero Motors that survived for 26 long years. On the other extreme, we have an example of the alliance between Bajaj and Renault–Nissan that failed miserably at the onset without creating any value for the organizations. The foreign partner might decide to acquire the Indian organization's stake in the joint venture, as in the case of the alliance between IBM and Tata Consulting Services. It may be the other way round, with the Indian organization buying the foreign partner's stake, as it happened in the joint venture formed between TVS Motors and Suzuki, Japan.

Although the evolution of alliances will be driven by the strengths and weaknesses of the partners, there are two factors that influence the sustainability and likely direction of an alliance: the aspirations and the will to control the venture and relative contributions. If the global partner aspires full control of the venture and has learned the tricks of the trade in the local market, it would ultimately lead to an acquisition or dissolution of the alliance. On the other hand, if the local player harbors global ambitions and has the confidence to compete on its own against the multinational, it would lead to a conflict.

The Road Ahead: Lifecycle of a Typical Strategic Alliance

As illustrated in Figure 1.6, a typical strategic alliance starts with having clarity with respect to the business case, going ahead with selecting a partner, negotiating the terms and conditions of the alliance, managing the alliance, and lastly, assessing the performance of the alliance. The subsequent chapters in the book take us through each stage of the alliance lifecycle, wherein we deliberate on some important characteristics of each stage. The spotlight will be trained on the foremost question: What decisions should executives take to create value from the alliance?

The mission of the book is to provide a solid overview of what every business student or a management executive needs to know with respect to the formation and management of a strategic alliance. The content will be taken forward by connecting to examples of strategic alliances between organizations.

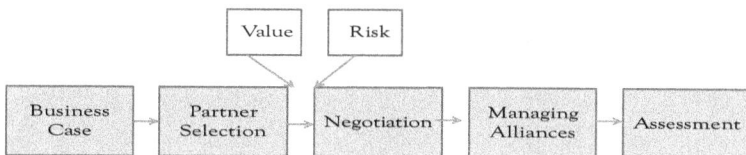

Figure 1.6 A representation of a typical alliance lifecycle

CHAPTER 2

Business Case for an Alliance

Having clarity of the business case or the reason for taking a strategic decision to enter into an alliance forms the heart and soul of an alliance that creates value for an organization. But, exactly, what is involved in having clarity on the business case for an alliance? What are some of the critical questions that an executive needs to answer to have a conviction on the business case? In this chapter, the author presents an overview of some of the important decisions. Like any other strategic decision, the decision to enter into an alliance is rooted in having a comprehensive understanding of the organization's external and internal environment. At the outset, an organization's executives should wrestle with the issue of what the critical success factors in the industry are and what capabilities are required for an organization to succeed. Organizations have the choice to grow internally through the process of capability-building, or externally through resource-picking. A couple of questions that the executive would be required to handle are: Are the capabilities available internally with the organization? If not, can the organization develop them internally? If not, are the capabilities available with other organizations? How to get access to the capabilities? Knowing the capabilities cannot be developed internally and are available with other organizations the organization has a choice—to acquire the organization that has the capabilities or get into an alliance with the other organization.

Generally, the more distant a business opportunity is from the core competencies and existing businesses, the more likely an organization would consider an alliance instead of an acquisition or organic growth.

What Does Business Case Deliberation Entail?

The process of determining the business case consists of four integrated decisions:

1. Understanding the strategic importance of the alliance.
2. Questioning whether the organization is ready to get into an alliance.
3. Deliberating the correctness of the timing of the decision.
4. Deliberating the commitment to the alliance.

Figure 2.1 displays the four-task deliberation, which will be examined in detail next:

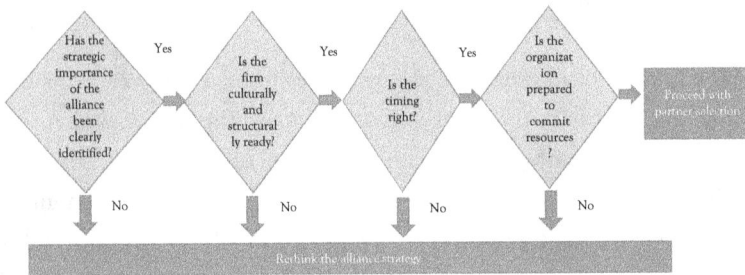

Figure 2.1 Business case deliberation

Decision Set 1: Understanding the Strategic Importance of the Alliance

As a first step, it is important for management executives to understand the strategic importance of the alliance. The corporate or business strategy of an organization or division should mold its alliance strategy. The executive should have a clear understanding of the organization's strategy and the overall objectives established. The organization might be facing capability gaps in meeting the objectives identified. An understanding of why an alliance the best alternative is very important. Also, an understanding of what an alliance will help the organization achieve and how it would support the overall strategy is important. An alliance might range from scale alliances to scope alliances. Whereas a scale alliance helps an organization achieve scale of operations, a scope alliance helps to diversify scope of operations. Organizations might collude together to increase the market power, which is a case of a collusive alliance. Organizations at similar points in the value network might combine their distinctive capabilities to form complementary alliances. A strategic alliance has little value for an organization if it does not help the organization achieve its strategic objectives. From a resource-based perspective, it is a well-accepted fact that alliance partners seek resources that are complementary to their own; resource complementarity leads to value creation. For example, in the case of an international strategic alliance, the organization-specific resources of the international organization complement the market-specific resources of the local partner.

The industry lifecycle to an extent determines the business case for an alliance. While in the introduction stage, partners come together to explore new avenues for growth, in the maturity stage, gaining scale economies for efficient operations may be top priority of the partners.

There are various motives that drive organizations toward collaboration. Spreading or reducing costs, avoiding or countering competition, learning from other companies, and securing vertical and horizontal linkages are some of the general motives. Organizations venturing into international locations, in addition to minimizing exposure in risky environments, look forward to gaining location-specific assets and overcoming legal constraints by getting into an alliance with an international partner. These motives help to strengthen the business case for the alliance.

Another way to classify the underlying motivation for getting into a strategic alliance is by identifying the location of the motive, that is, internal or external to the organization, as well as the power of the motive, that is, opportunity (plus) or problem (negative). An alliance gives an organization an opportunity to exploit any excess capacity, have a better control over distribution outlets, gain customer or brand loyalty, and to explore a new product concept or a new process technology. An alliance also enables an organization to overcome problems like inefficient production, technology stagnation, lack of adequate capital to compete, obsolete or low-quality product offering, decline in market share, threat of potential takeover, increased cost of supply, and intervention by the government.

Broadly, two set of motivations that can form the business case of an alliance are efficiency and effectiveness. Efficiency objectives of an organization, entailing *to do things right* involve the opportunities to reduce cost by forming alliances with organizations that have complementary expertise. To *do the right thing* or the effectiveness objectives of an organization involve market-based motivations to increase size and market share, or to create barriers to competitive entry. For example, Australian Open decided to partner with Infosys to deliver a unique, innovative, and enriching experience to the fans. Craig Tiley, Tournament Director, Australian Open, commented, "Partnering with Infosys is an exciting next step in our ongoing quest to innovate the Australian Open and engage new audiences across the world."[1]

The strategic importance might vary from one alliance to the other. For example, a cobranding alliance as that between Disney and McDonalds helps both partners:

- Access each other's marketing infrastructure
- Share marketing costs across the partners
- Reduce challenges of new product development
- Improve image and credibility of the product

However, risk of negative brand spillover can reduce the flexibility that a partner might have.

In the alliance between Schneider Electric and Tricolite Electrical Industries Ltd., Schneider was driven by the following factors:

- Overcome limited manufacturing capability
- Share risk
- Capitalize on the growing Indian market
- Enhance product offerings to customers

On the other hand, Tricolite through the alliance:
- Got associated with a global player
- Gained the latest technology
- Enhanced its brand image

---

[1] PTI New Delhi. September 10, 2018. "Infosys Inks Deal with Australian Open as Official Digital Innovation Partner." https://thehindubusinessline.com/info-tech/infosys-inks-deal-with-australian-open-as-official-digital-innovation-partner/article24916618.ece (accessed September 26, 2019)

- Expanded customer base
- Created customer value

For a public sector power generation organization, National Thermal Power Corporation (NTPC), manufacturing of equipment was never its forte. Getting into an alliance with Bharat Heavy Electricals Ltd. (BHEL) for manufacturing and supply of power plant equipment was a sound business case.

Decision Set 2: Questioning Whether the Organization Is Ready to Get Into an Alliance

Past Experience in Collaboration

Organizations differ with respect to their experience in alliances. An organization having created value through an alliance would prefer to get into another alliance as compared to an organization that has failed in a previous alliance. Companies like Cargill Foods, Facebook, and so on that have met various strategic objectives by acquiring smaller organizations might not be able to manage an alliance and create value through an alliance. An acquisition strategy might work out better for these organizations. In fact, a senior executive very rightly said, "If you are good at collaborating inside the company, you will be good at collaborating outside."

Established Organizational Practices

A strategic alliance demands incentive and appraisal systems that are very distinct from an organization that operates independently. Management executives when deliberating on an alliance need to be convinced that the organizational practices are designed to suit the needs of working in an alliance. An example to the aforementioned is the case of an alliance that has employees deputed to the alliance organization as part of an agreement. The HR rules of the organization should have a provision for redeploying the employees in the parent organization in case of failure and dissolution of the alliance organization. Or, in fact, when hiring, potential employees could be quizzed intently with respect to how they would behave in a cooperative environment.

Nike, as an organization, promotes extensive internal collaboration. The organization has been broken into categories, and a connect is maintained between the different categories. Collaborative tools like WebEx and video conferencing are used in a major way. The organization also understands the importance of maintaining dialogue with customers.

System of Healthy Communication

The foundation of a strong strategic alliance lies on trust between the partner organizations. A healthy system of communication is critical to build trust among members. Organizations equipped with healthy and robust internal and external communication mechanisms are better placed with respect to managing alliances. If partners are involved in technical work, communication between partners is very critical for efficient functioning of the organization. If the product is designed strictly for exports, it is less critical to understand the demands of the local government *vis-à-vis* where the products are being produced for the local market. In this case, the competition is with local organizations, and it is critical to interact smoothly with local regulators and government officials. For success of a joint venture, it is very essential to have trust and a good working relationship between parties, something which is very difficult to accomplish when the partners have unstated knowledge goals.

Promoting Team-Based Work

The organizational culture with respect to recognizing team versus individual work and performance is an important factor that needs to be considered when deliberating on a decision to get into an alliance. An alliance thrives on team or collaborative efforts, and an organization that has a culture of team-based work is able to create more value from an alliance. In fact, an international joint venture involves a tripartite relationship, involving the international joint venture, the foreign parent, and the local parent. A culture that supports such a multifaceted relationship is in a better position to create value out of an alliance.

Project Management or Technical and Relational Skills

An alliance not only requires executives with in-depth technical skills, but also executives that have strong interpersonal and relational skills. Organizations having such employees on the rolls are able to leverage them to create value from the alliance. For example, when India Cables Ltd. was deliberating on getting into an alliance with Nippon of Japan, they inducted a retired Japanese senior-level executive into their organization. The Japanese executive was required to help India Cables Ltd. build relationship with Nippon and take the alliance forward. An alliance is a project that has to be managed according to the various milestones established. For example, Renault was able to create value from its alliance with Nissan by leveraging the alliance management skills that Carlos Ghosn had.

Decision Set 3: Deliberating the Correctness of the Timing of the Decision

Like any other strategic decision, timing of the decision to get into a strategic alliance is critical. Management executives need to deliberate on whether the organization can afford postponing the decision of getting into an alliance. A question they need to answer: What is the opportunity cost of foregoing an alliance? Many times, organizations get into an alliance to pre-empt similar moves of competitors. In trying to balance the risks of premature entry and the costs of missed opportunities, organizations that value the net potential as high will have a strong drive to enter into a partnership than those who value it low.

Decision Set 4: Deliberating the Commitment to the Alliance

The decision to get into an alliance might divide an organization's focus on its core operations. Management executives before taking the decision forward need to be convinced that the core operations are not put at risk because of the alliance. An alliance to be successful needs support from various stakeholders—the board, the top management, and the employees. Only when the management executives are convinced that the organization is ready to commit resources to the alliance, should they go ahead with the alliance.

When an organization enters into a strategic alliance, which is related to its business, it leads to creation of more value than entering into an unrelated area. This is because it can exploit its core competencies, leading to economies of scale and scope, efficiency in resource allocation, and opportunities to use particular technical and managerial skills.

Organizations enter into alliances when the perceived benefits from the alliance outweigh the perceived costs. As the environment and circumstances surrounding the venture and its partners change, each organization's cost–benefit ratio also changes. When the ratio for either shifts such that continued participation is viewed as a net cost and not a net benefit, that organization–being economically rational–will seek to terminate the alliance.

An interesting question here is: *Can a business case contribute to the failure of an alliance?* There can be multiple scenarios wherein strategic planning or having a business case can contribute to the failure of an alliance: (i) organizations may prematurely enter into an alliance driven more by actions of competitors, (ii) no strategy has been laid down with respect to prioritization of the alliance among its portfolio of alliances, (iii) organizations' failure to invest in the competence or function of the alliance, and (iv) ambiguous performance expectation.

Figure 2.2 illustrates the importance of having a sound business case for an alliance.

In essence, strategy must lie at the heart of every alliance. Management executives who try to close an alliance deal without being sensitive of how critical the deal is for the organization's strategy would not create value. The rationale for inter-organizational collaboration changes over time. It is, therefore, important for executives to continuously reflect on the strategy and analyze it. It is also important for management executives to understand that an organization has a portfolio of alliances, and organizations need to conduct regular audits of these portfolios to identify the gaps that serve as a strong business case for future alliances.

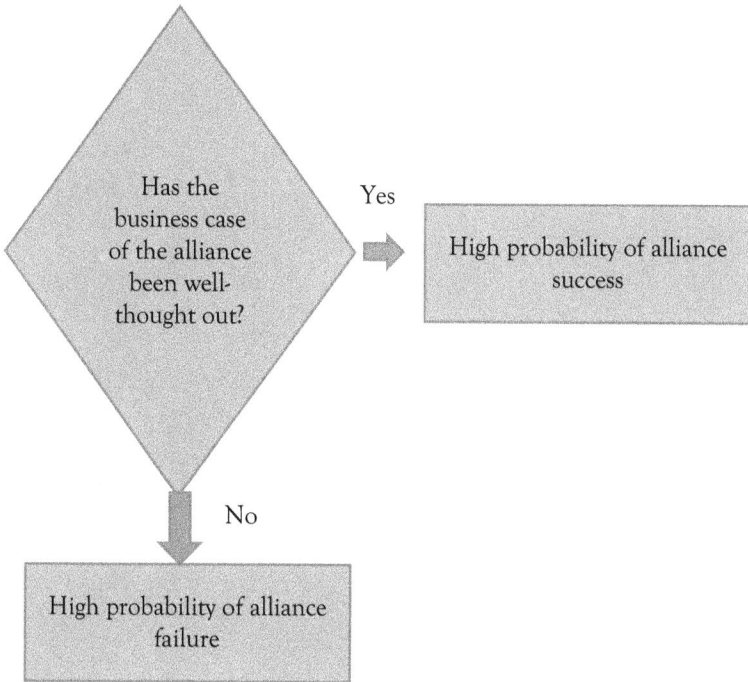

Figure 2.2 Business case outcomes

CHAPTER 3

Selecting a Partner for an Alliance

Once the organization is clear with the strategy and the business case for the alliance, it is important to identify and choose a partner. In the current age of aggressive competition, the competitive edge of organizations might also be determined by the close cooperation and solid relationships with external organizations. Many times, during strategic analysis, likely partners may have come to the fore, but it is important to evaluate explicitly what the partner contributes to the alliance. An organization can seek out a partner for its operations or it can respond to a proposal from another organization to collaborate with it. In either case, it is essential to assess the potential partner not only for the resources it can contribute, but also the motivation and willingness the partner has to collaborate.

Organizations tend to lack discipline with respect to performing this step.

There are five main reasons why strategic alliances fail, as illustrated in Figure 3.1.

As can be seen from the preceding figure, four out of five reasons for failure of alliances are pertaining to selection of a partner. There could be a misfit with the strategy of the partner, there might be cultural differences, lack of trust, or partner unable to deliver expected competences. Organizations living in a particular country tend to share similar values, and they bring these values to their alliances. Hence, organizations' values are a reflection of the culture of the nation. International joint ventures, involving organizations from different countries, tend to have different values. These differences in values make it more tough for international joint venture partners to have a consensus on common goals, solutions

Five main reasons for alliance failure (%)

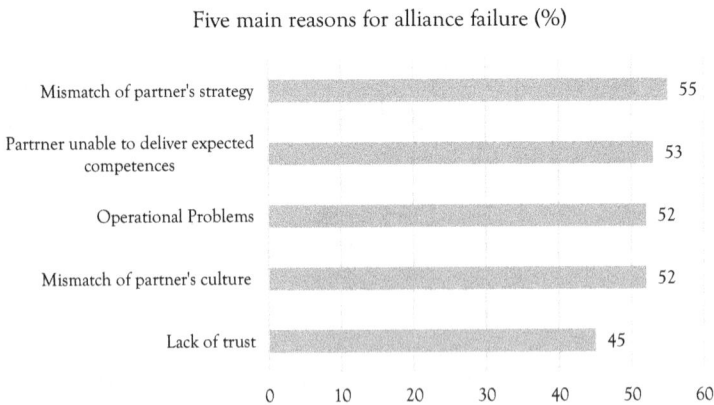

Figure 3.1 Reasons for alliance failure

Source: Duisters, D., G. Duysters, and A.P. de Man. December 2011. "A Study into the Role of a Partner Selection Process in Alliance Capability Building." pp. 775–783 https://pdfs.semantic-scholar.org/9012/3c1206021d1f9b149c3de686ac0d959d40a6.pdf,

to problems, and resolution to conflicts than if they came from the same country.

Differences in corporate cultures may also lead to differences in organizational practices resulting in conflicting behaviors, further leading to misunderstandings and differences in dealing with each other. Partners with different corporate cultures may spend time and energy to establish mutually agreeable managerial practices, thereby incurring higher costs and mistrust. Therefore, when selecting a partner, organizations should deal with each other's strategy, culture, trust, competencies, and expectations.

It is argued that the success rate of strategic alliances would improve if organizations follow systematic and analytical methods for partner selection. Only if the organization-specific advantages of the partners are compatible, the cooperation will lead to additional cost reducing or differentiation enhancing potential. Culture and trust play a very important role with respect to partner selection. A good track record at times serves as an alternative to stringent control mechanisms. Demand for dominant control, on the contrary, hints toward lack of trust.

An important question here is who can be my potential partner? This depends on the business purpose for which the alliance is getting formed. Aditya Birla Capital (ABCL) and the U.S. firm Varde Partners formed an exclusive joint venture partnership to invest one billion U.S. dollars, approximately 70 billion U.S. dollars in stressed assets in India. According to Ajay Srinivasan, chief executive of ABCL:

> The Asset Reconstruction (ARC) business is a strong addition to the businesses we already have at ABCL. We see a large opportunity in the distressed space, especially in the mid-corporate segment. One of the things that we bring to the table as a group is that we understand how to run many businesses. Thus, our decision to enter into a joint venture with Värde Partners, who bring restructuring expertise to augment our core strength.

Ilfryn Carstairs, co-CIO of Värde Partners, complemented by saying:

> We see India as a core market for Värde and a critical part of our long-term strategy in Asia. We are particularly excited to partner

with an organization with the quality reputation and established relationships of ABCL to address what we believe will be a very large, multi-year opportunity. Värde's deep, global restructuring expertise developed over the firm's 25-year history will be complemented by Aditya Birla's strong team and experience in Indian credit and asset markets.[1]

A partner can be a supplier, a customer, a complementor, or even a competitor. Potential partners can be identified by monitoring journals, attending technical conferences, participating in social activities, and by developing links with academic institutions. Developing contacts with managers of a focal organization may pave the route for subsequent introductions to managers of other organizations.

Developing the Criteria for Partner Selection

It is important for management executives to develop a partner selection criterion that can be used for shortlisting of potential partners. The motivation or the business case of the alliance will also determine the selection criterion of partners. The criteria shown in Table 3.1 can serve as a guide for selection of a partner. Strategic fit can be defined as "the extent to which alliance partners have congruent organization-level strategies, as well as compatible strategies for the alliance itself, and the strengths and capabilities of the partners form a synergy within the alliance." Cultural fit "refers to the harmony of organizational philosophies, goals, and values between alliance partners." Organizational fit "is the in the extent of similarity partners' organizational capabilities, such as processes and organizational design" (Sarkar et al. 2001; Swoboda et al. 2011).

It is important to keep in mind that the criteria managers use for selection of partners might vary with the kind of alliance project. Also, the institutional environments at work in different economies might lead to differences in the partner selection criterion. For example, Chinese,

[1]   Chatterjee, D. 2019. "Aditya Birla, US Firm Varde Partners in $1 billion JV for Stressed Assets." August 30, 2018, https://business-standard.com/article/companies/aditya-birla-us-firm-v%C3%A4rde-partners-in-1-billion-jv-for-stressed-assets-118083000065_1.html (accessed July 30, 2019)

Table 3.1 Criteria for partner selection

Criteria	Deliberation
Strategic fit or compatibility of goals	• Is there a fit with the partner with respect to the need to get access to the product or geography? • Is there a fit with respect to access to technology and need for knowledge of the local market? • Is there a fit with respect to a shorter time to market and generating cash?
Capability fit or complementarity capabilities	• Do we complement each other with respect to the product and market? • Do we complement each other with respect to the technology and capital? • Do we complement each other with respect to access to local customers and developing a global network?
Cultural fit	• Is there a fit in our corporate culture? • Is there a fit in the industry culture? • Is there a fit in the national culture?
Organizational fit	• How similar or different are our decision-making styles? • How similar or different are our practices with respect to documentation of policies? • Do we follow similar approach to accounting and reporting? • Do we follow a similar approach to giving incentives?
Conflict of interest	• Do our geographical markets overlap? • Do we compete for the same resources required for production? • What can be the probable differences over transfer pricing? • What can be the probable differences in our growth agenda? • Does the partner have a relationship with our competitors or friends or allies?

Source: Bamford, J. D., B. Gomes-Casseres, and M.S. Robinson. 2003. "Putting Strategy before Structure."*In Mastering Alliance Strategy: A Comprehensive Guide to Design, Management, and Organization*, 63-74. John Wiley and Sons Inc

Indian, and Russian organizations might differ with respect to their preferences for alliance partners. Multinational organizations might, therefore, be required to adapt their approach to establishing alliances in different countries.

An important question at this stage is: *Is it important to assess the relationship fit?* Yes. Practice has found that organizations that take time to evaluate the relationship fit tend to be more successful in building and managing strong alliances. Organizations relying on intuition for relationship fit fail with respect to selecting the right partner. But, how to assess relationship fit with potential partners? Decision-making processes, escalation procedures, approach to problem-solving, business practices, and information-sharing standards can be used as surrogate measures of relationship fit. As majority of the organizations lack an established method for evaluating these relationship issues, they often neglect assessing this fit and rely on gut feeling when selecting a partner. While there are many reasons leading to the failure of alliances, a critical one is insufficient relational harmony to overcome conflicts and opportunistic behaviors inherent in all alliance settings.

Organizations, however, need to keep in mind that a dynamic technology environment might reduce the fit among partners, thereby making the benefits from the alliances superfluous. High market uncertainty increases the difficulty level of managing diverse resources. For example, in the early 2000s, the competitive position of IBM Microelectronics was threatened due to the rapid changes in the industry structure that was moving toward modularization. The pressure from the external environment drove IBM to experiment with a number of developmental alliances.

An important factor that management executives should pay attention in case of partner selection is the second- or third-order connections, that is, connections between the partner and third-party firms. It is important to take a broader view of the connections within the industry.

For example, Cisco lays down specific criteria for selection of partners. To name a few:

1. The potential for the alliance to generate revenue and value for the customers
2. The commitment toward the alliance of the chief executive officer and the strategy vice president
3. Adequate high level of investment in capital, people, and intellectual property
4. A minimal product or service overlap, wherein the company believed that a portfolio overlap of more than 20 percent of revenue or a

direct distribution channel led to conflict that made the alliance nonstrategic

Similarly, the following partner selection criteria was laid down by Schneider Electric when it was in search for a partner in India:

- Annual turnover of more than 30 crores
- To have own manufacturing of switchboards
- In-house sales, engineering, and design team
- Interested in systems program
- To have a national presence
- Not to be committed to any competitor of Schneider

In the case of National Thermal Power Corporation, trust in relationships that it had established with Bharat Heavy Electricals Ltd. and Coal India Limited in previous alliances guided it in partner selection in subsequent alliances too. The inter-dependence and ties established in prior alliances increase the probability of alliances with previous partners. Government, however, plays a critical role in the alliances formed and partners selected by public sector undertakings.

It can be mentioned that when selecting a partner, an effort to combine similar resources might lead to the failure of the alliance. Complementary resources and capabilities between partners contribute to alliance stability. Organizations, however, need to decide on the level of diversity among partners. Although high levels of diversity increase the potential for learning, such diversity also leads to increased coordination difficulty. Also, selecting partners having a long-term orientation is helpful for the alliance, as it gives the partners the ability to overcome challenges, resolve conflicts, and continue under uncertainty.

Generally, organizations sought similarly sized organizations as partners, the rationale being that by selecting a similarly sized partner, a company could be assured that the two placed the alliance in about the same importance. Also, both the organizations would be in near-equal power positions for bargaining. Developed market organizations search out for partners that provide legitimacy in local markets where the former might not have still built reputation required to compete successfully. Similarly, emerging market organizations, as they lack the absorptive capacity to learn new capabilities, look out for partners that will help them to learn and then transfer the required knowledge. Organizations might at times have second thoughts with respect to search for a large established player, fearing that it might lengthen the timeframe for achieving the objectives. This gets reflected through a comment made by the president of a pharma technology company:

> In a large company, it takes a long time to figure out whom you have to talk to; find the right people with decision-making authority. You need to be assured of proper diligence and movement, or your deal will get lost. It might make sense to look at an intermediate company to co-develop the technology, rather than going right away to a multinational company.[2]

Does the industry lifecycle influence an organization's identification of a potential partner? Probable yes. When an industry is in the exploratory stage, the strength of resources with an incumbent organization might not hold as much an importance as the aspiration level of the firm to innovate and explore new avenues for growth. Therefore, in such a stage of the industry lifecycle, it makes sense for an organization to seek out a partner whose aspiration levels are very strong. However, industries in the development stage would require an optimal combination of aspirations and resources. For example, the automobile industry, which saw a disruption due to the advent of electric and self-driving technology, saw players like Ford Motors and Mahindra getting into an alliance to fight competition from technology-based firms. The alliance would enable Ford to leverage Mahindra's distribution reach within India and Mahindra aspiring to benefit from Ford's reach in other emerging markets. According to Jim Farley, the Ford executive vice-president and president of global markets:

> Ford is committed to India and this alliance can help us deliver the best vehicles and services to customers while profitably grow-

---

[2]   Herbert, J. 2004. *Pharma Technologies Inc.* Ivey Management Services.

ing in the world's fifth largest vehicle market." The company had invested over two billion U.S. dollars in India and planned to spend more to set up an engineering center that would help to manufacture products for the local market and in accordance to the changing customer trends.[3]

When innovation is the primary motive of the partners, getting into an alliance with novel partners carries the risk of free-riding on the investments made by the firm in current alliances, thereby eroding the value of hierarchical alliances. Common skills, shared languages, and similar cognitive structures enable partners to communicate and learn from each other. For example, IBM's choice of partners in its various exploratory alliances was driven by a reputation that the players carried with respect to their willingness to cooperate and the surety that they would act in a responsible manner with respect to the intellectual property of other firms.

It has also been noticed that collaborating with diverse partners on a narrow range of activities in the value chain results in higher level of innovation than spreading widely across the value chain. For example, General Motors entered into a diverse portfolio of alliances. The range of its portfolios was alliance with suppliers of various automobile components; alliances with the small car manufacturers like Isuzu, Daewoo, Suzuki, and Nissan; and alliance with Fanuc for robotics technology and with Toyota to learn about the production system. General Motors failed to create value out of the various alliances.

Soliciting a Partner

Based on the selection criteria developed by the executives, potential partners are identified and shortlisted. This is followed by a due diligence exercise, with respect to the share of the market held by the prospective partner and the rate of growth in the business of the prospective partner,

---

[3] Reuters. 2017. "Ford Motors and Mahindra Join Hands in a Strategic Alliance to Face Rivals." September 18, 2017, https://firstpost.com/auto/features-auto/ford-motors-and-mahindra-join-hands-in-a-strategic-alliance-to-face-rivals-4056611.html (accessed August 28, 2019)

on the shortlisted partners. Common practice in many industries is to give mandates to intermediaries to conduct the due diligence before proceeding further.

The next task is to solicit or put forth the idea of an alliance to the potential partners. The question is who does this task for you. In case of private sector organizations, seminars and high-level dinners frequented by the top brass set the foundation for prospective strategic alliances. The heads of companies, after building a camaraderie, evaluate the potential of working together on a common strategic agenda.

In case of public sector organizations, many times, entry into strategic alliances happens through the formal process of bidding. Bids are invited from interested players. After a round of technical evaluation, commercial bids are invited with the player quoting the lowest identified as the suitable partner.

Finalizing the Strategic Partner

In order to finalize the potential partner, it is important that the partner is convinced with the unique selling proposition of your organization. At times, leveraging others, say consultants and advisors, third-party endorsements by media, can do the task. An organization can increase its visibility by participating in trade fairs, by distributing brochures, and by fostering contacts in the locale of potential collaboration. It is also important to identify the gatekeepers, that is, corporate and government authorities that might block the deal. In emerging economies, where a multinational has to complete a number of legal formalities before it becomes entitled to doing business, the network that the local player has with the regulatory bodies and other legal authorities can serve as a unique selling proposition for the local player.

The key question in front of management executives now is: *Can we expect the partner to be a mirror image of ourselves?* No, probably not. It is imperative that executives identify the differences and develop a plan for dealing with them.

Also, executives need to keep in mind that a partner selected also implies a set of potential partners that have not got chosen. How will they feel about the new positioning in the industry?

Organizations might be forced to form alliances with partners that are not trusted. In such a scenario, it becomes imperative that comprehensive formal contracts and appropriate controls are in place. Many times, prior ties can be used to operationalize trust. In fact, a dilemma for many organizations is: *Should I get into an alliance with whom I have a prior alliance experience or look out for a new partner?* For example, Maruti Suzuki India Ltd.'s choice of Inergy Automotive as an alliance partner was driven not only by the plastic technology that Inergy had, but also because Inergy was already a supplier to the parent company in Japan.

A question to deliberate: *Does it make sense to ally with a partner weak in resource endowments?* Probably yes, if the partner's strategic aspirations are strongly aligned with that of the firm. For example, does it make sense to ally with Coca Cola because it has a very strong distribution system? The probability is high that Coca Cola might not be interested in deploying its distribution network to support your entry into the market. However, it may make sense to ally with a partner who has a sufficiently good distribution system if the organization truly intends to deploy its skills for the benefit of the alliance. It is rightly said that organizations should seek partners whose strategic goals converge, while their competitive goals diverge.

Figure 3.2 illustrates the importance of choosing the right partner for the alliance. From the preceding discussion, it is evident that it is of vital importance to select the right partners that will help in minimization of the total cost of production, as well as maximization of profits and the quality of products. Organizations need to be particular about selecting partners that are strong, either financially or with respect to the desired resources. An alliance between two strong partners has a greater success rate than that of an alliance wherein even one of the partners is weak. If management executives spend time in fixing a weak core business, their attention and focus on the alliance will be at stake. Also, one needs to keep in mind that by getting into an alliance, an organization has less autonomy as compared to an acquisition. An organization is not able to control everything because of the existence of its alliance partner. This control gap can be overcome by choosing the right partner.

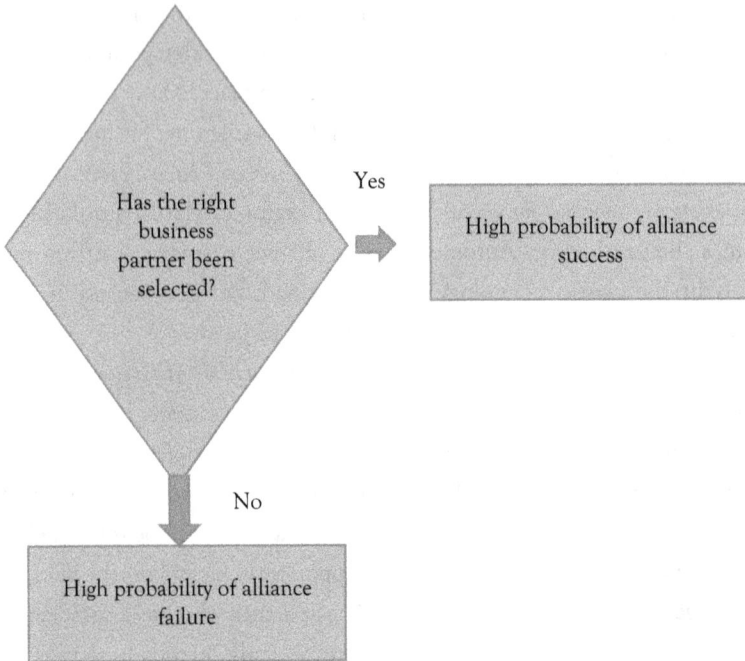

Figure 3.2 Partner selection outcomes

CHAPTER 4

Assessing Individual and Joint Values

"Agreed; we both hate the cat. I'm just unsure what else you will bring to the partnership"

Before moving to the next stage of negotiations, management executives need to be convinced with respect to the individual and joint values anticipated from the alliance. An alliance will create value for the partners and be considered to be successful if both partners are able to achieve their strategic objectives and are able to earn a return that is equal to or greater than the cost of capital over the life of the alliance.

The value or success of any strategy, including alliances, is in terms of its impact on profitability of the organization, with profitability getting impacted by three possible ways: (i) increase in unit sales, (ii) increase in unit price that customers will pay, and (iii) lowering of its average cost per unit.

What Do We Understand by the Term Value?

As illustrated in Figure 4.1, the term *value* may be looked at differently by different partners.

Organizations attaching a financial value to the alliance measure it through return on investment both in the short and long term. Value of an alliance can also be looked at from the perspective of control over supply of components. A short-term measure would require assessment with respect to any cost savings made by routing the component through the alliance. A long-term measure would require an assessment of improvement in component performance over the years. For example, Fiat's production facility in Cincinnati has multiple vendors working under the same roof. Employees of the different organizations interact with one another. Does not the preceding arrangement add value for both Fiat and the vendors, both in the short and long run?

Alliances with suppliers and close coordination for sharing information and promoting supplier development play an important role in specialized industries like aircraft manufacturing. Such kinds of close vertical ties, involving rich exchange of information and close commitment between partners, lead to greater joint activities between partners

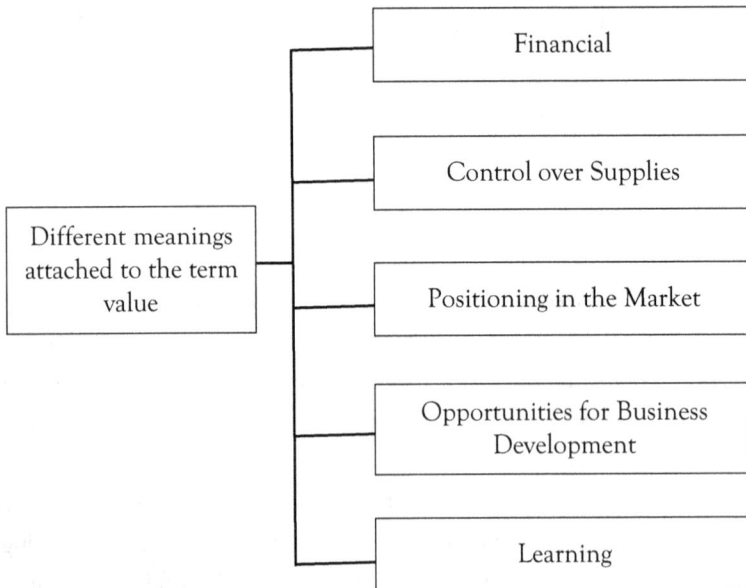

Figure 4.1 Value anticipated from an alliance

and greater investment in assets translate to value for the partners. An example from the automobile industry is that of Toyota's alliance with its suppliers. The organization turns traditional buyer–supplier relationships into trust-based partnerships using supplier development programs to help its suppliers improve their performance. This results in better quality for Toyota's products. These improvements also lead to higher prices that consumers are willing to pay.

Another perspective of looking at value is in terms of position in the market in lieu of the alliance. In the short run, an alliance might help the partners to increase market share, but in the long run, the alliance might help companies have customers who are loyal to their brand. In the case of Hero Motors and Honda, the fuel-efficient motorbikes enabled the partners to immediately capture a market share more than their peers. But, it was working in the alliance for a long term that enabled Honda to have a set of customers who were loyal to its brand.

Many organizations attach value to an alliance not only on the basis of growth opportunities given by the alliance, but also whether the alliance has set in motion the choice of exploring other strategic opportunities with the partner in the long run. For example, the alliance between Fiat and Tata in India started as a sales and distribution agreement wherein Fiat would use Tata's showrooms and distribution touchpoints for the sale of Fiat cars. Although this alliance created no value for Fiat, it gave both the partners an opportunity to jointly share their plant capacity for production of cars.

Where learning is the primary objective of the alliance, organizations attach value to getting access to the intellectual property rights of the technology owned by the other partner in the short run. Learning is much more than the acquisition of resources and includes building the capabilities of an organization. In the long run, value is attached to whether working in the alliance has led to development of technological capability or improvement in the research and development (R&D) cycle times. The alliance between Honda and Hero Motors gave Hero the access to Honda's engine technology in the short run, but in the long run, the true test was if Hero Motors was much more self-sufficient with respect to technology development. To a great extent, the extent of learning is dependent on the absorptive capacity of either of the partners. With time, a joint venture takes on characteristics that are unique and independent of the respective parent organizations. More so in the case of an international joint venture that adapts itself to suit the needs of the local market. The absorptive capacity of an international joint venture can be defined as its ability to evaluate resources from local and foreign partners, integrate the acquired resources, and apply the pooled resources to suit the needs of the local market.

In order to have a clarity with respect to how to measure performance, it is important for management executives to have a clarity on the fundamental question: What is the alliance trying to achieve? The performance metrics or the anticipated value from the alliance should be linked to the strategic intent of the alliance, be measurable, and should be communicated well to the relevant stakeholders. An improper assessment of the value and identification of the measurement metrics might lead to faulty evaluation of the outcome of the alliance, and henceforth a wrong decision with respect to the future of the alliance.

At times, governments require multinational enterprises to enter into a joint venture with local players; this can alter the dynamics of a joint venture relationship and thereby distort a joint venture's economic potential.

An overlap between the products and markets of the partner firms has the potential to generate scale and scope economies and also lower the cost of organizing resources. However, an overlap between the scope of operations of partner firms has a potential for opportunism, which can negate any potential gain from a synergistic combination of resources of partner. Similarly, an overlap between the value chain activities of the partner firm may make the activities vulnerable to competitive imitation. It increases the need for coordination among partners. If it makes the partners more vulnerable to opportunistic exploitation, it raises the overall transaction costs, which might have unfavorable implication for value creation. In case of alliance networks, value created would be dependent on the supplementary and complementary resources accessed through multiple simultaneous alliances with multiple partners.

Management executives might like to ponder on: *Do differences in size between alliance partners matter?* Differences in size of partners lead to differences in the costs of implementing alliance plans as the administrative systems and procedures of large organizations differ from that of smaller ones. These differences might lead to dissimilar approaches in the alliance management, which might put at risk the value created for the alliance parents. A larger partner might also try to dominate a smaller partner. On the other hand, a smaller partner might also benefit from the brand name and expertise of the larger partner. The importance that partners give to an alliance might also crop up because of differences in size. For example, if the alliance is between a large and a small organization, the alliance comprises a large size of operations for the smaller organization, leading to a high possibility of the latter taking more interest in the alliance.

Value created for shareholders is also influenced by the partners' ownership positions. Ownership structure hints at the bargaining power that each partner has. Equal ownership might lead to coordination challenges and potential conflicts between the partners. It might also increase organizational complexity of managing joint ventures.

Also, shareholder value creation in case of alliances between competitors is significantly lower than those involved in noncompetitor alliances. Why is it so? Probably, because of the huge transaction costs involved in gaining commitment to an alliance between direct competitors. However, a good governance structure involving competing partners can help to share development costs, along with access to cross pipeline expertise.

Pointers for Management Executives

Mentioned next are a few pointers for management executives.

Alliances Can Lead To Both Creation And Destruction Of Value

An alliance that achieves the objective for which it has been formed adds value to the partners. An alliance can also destroy value for its partners. As we are all aware, an alliance increases dependence on the partner for the resource or capability and inhibits a company from developing its own capability. An alliance that terminates without value creation might lead to a partner fending for itself. However, one needs to be cognizant of the fact that the value created or destroyed might not apply uniformly to both the partners.

Being Good At One Kind Of Alliance Does Not Automatically Mean That An Organization Will Be Good At Another Kind Of Alliance

Managing a joint venture that involves partners working together in close proximity requires a skillset that is very different from managing a contractual alliance. Management executives should, therefore, not be under the false impression that if a contractual alliance in the past has created value for the organization, a joint venture would likewise do.

Strong Firm Management Does Not Imply Success Of The Alliance

With purpose of each alliance being different and alliances involving different partners, each alliance is unique. A strong management team does not warrant a 100 percent probability of success. The alliance between Renault and Nissan has been successful, but the same management when got into an alliance with Bajaj in India, it was a failure. What went wrong?

Certain Alliance Types Create Value In One Industry, But Not In Another

Management executives have a choice with respect to the alliance structure. All types of alliances might not be applicable for all industries. For example, in the retail industry, majority of players enter into simple franchising arrangements, *vis-à-vis* an automobile or a pharmaceutical industry where joint ventures are more predominant. It is important to maintain a fit between strategy and structure to create value.

Value Of Shareholders Is Enhanced By Previous Alliance Experience

The aim of every organization is to increase the returns on investment so that the value disbursed to shareholders is enhanced. A company that is able to leverage its past experience of entering into and managing alliances is able to create more value from an alliance. In the case of Nippon, Japan, its experience of forming a joint venture had not been very good. Therefore, when it entered into an alliance with India Cables Ltd., it insisted on entering into a technical alliance that did not involve the legal formalities of setting up a separate joint venture company. As organizations accumulate cooperative experience, their increasing abilities to anticipate and respond to various contingencies are likely to enhance the chances of success in subsequent alliances. Organizations might, however, differ in their abilities to appropriate, capture, share, and disseminate knowledge from previous alliances.

Value Is Enhanced By Entering Into Alliances Linked To Core Business

When an organization enters into a joint venture, which is related to its business, it leads to creation of more value. This is because it can exploit its core competencies, leading to economies of scale and scope. It can allocate its resources more efficiently and also has opportunities to use particular technical and managerial skills.

Figure 4.2 illustrates the importance of having a clarity on the individual and joint values to be created in an alliance. It is clear that value creation in an alliance is dependent on the anticipated value appropriation by partners. In order to create value, it is essential to understand, redeploy, and utilize the pool of complementary resources. Any venture would continue till complementarity is maintained, and the venture leads to value creation for both the partners. Also, firms probably might not enter into a cooperative arrangement if they feel that the rewards they will garner within the arrangement are not proportionate to the value they contribute.

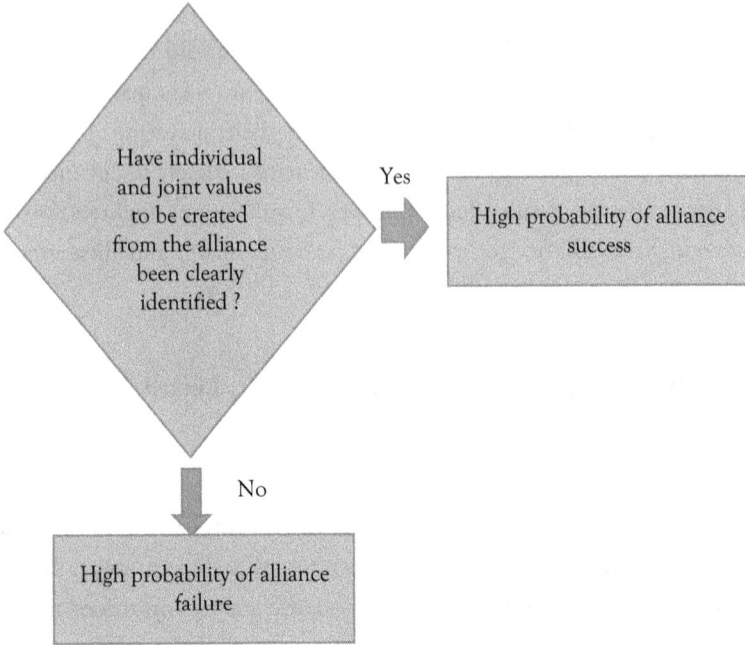

Figure 4.2 Identification of value outcome

CHAPTER 5

Assessing and Managing Risks

Organizations enter into multiple alliances to diversify the risk involved due to partial commitment by alliance partners. Alliances, by nature, are open-ended, and if not managed carefully, can nullify all the potential benefits from the alliance. Managing different kinds of risks in a strategic alliance is a complex task. Management executives, before they proceed to negotiate the alliance, need to assess the risks involved in the alliance. An inability to assess and manage the risks involved would lead to an unsteady alliance that devalues the organization. Strategic alliances can be seen as a risky strategy, success of which might often not be related to the efforts of the partner firms.

Consider the alliance between Tata Global Beverages and Starbucks Corporation that was set up as a 50:50 joint venture in October 2012.

India being primarily a tea-drinking country, with rising disposable income and a youth population, was seeing a shift toward drinking of coffee. Starbucks Corporation witnessing mature markets in other geographies saw India as a potential market for growth. Starbucks hoped to gain from the local knowledge and the presence of Tata in India. Tata, on the other hand, hoped to gain from the association with the iconic brand and also learn best practices in roasting of coffee beans. It was decided that the joint venture would source coffee beans from Tata Coffee (a subsidiary of Tata Global Beverages). Together, they also planned to work on premium tea, although, under a different agreement. Rivals Café Coffee Day, Barista Lavazza, and Costa Coffee had already made their presence felt in the country. Whereas Café Coffee Day had more than 1,500 stores, the other two had more than 100 stores by 2013. By 2018, the joint venture had increased the number of stores to 100. Although the operating profit in the fiscal 2018 increased from INR 3.84 crore a year back to INR 10.25 crore, the bottom line was still at a loss of INR 15.23 crore.[1]

The question is what are some of the risks that the joint venture faces?

Risks in International Alliances

Risks faced by partners in an alliance can be categorized into three:

Relational Risk

Relational risk is the risk of unsatisfactory inter-organization cooperation. It is concerned with the possibility of partner organizations lacking commitment to the alliance and their probable opportunistic behavior sabotaging the purpose of the alliance. In fact, the importance of personal relationship is very high in the early phase of the alliance. Consider the alliance between General Motors and Daewoo. In this case, the partner organizations were more interested in pursuing their individual motives

---

[1] Sumit, M. 2019. "Starbucks Operating Profit Trebles as Store Count Hits 100 Mark." June 13, 2018, https://dnaindia.com/business/report-starbucks-operating-profit-trebles-as-store-count-hits-100-mark-2624770 (accessed September 26, 2019)

rather than working for a common objective. General Motors was more concerned with driving costs down, whereas Daewoo was more interested in gaining a greater share of the local market. In the Tata–Starbucks alliance, either Tata Beverages or Starbucks could act in an opportunistic manner to use the information shared during the alliance to further their independent motives or other hidden agendas outside the alliance. Because such activities put at risk the alliance, relational risk is an important component of the overall risk in alliances. As control is partially ceded to one of the other partners, it adds complexity to the relationship. Relational risk is peculiar to strategic alliances, and strategic moves made by single firms are not subject to these risks.

One partner's capability to continue contributing the resources—technology, capital, or some other asset—may diminish over time as compared to the other partner's capability. This may cause a drag on the collaborative arrangement and might lead to disagreement between the partners.

When organizations pursue market opportunities on their own, there is not much needed to cooperate with others; therefore, the risk of unsatisfactory inter-organization cooperation is very low. In case of strategic alliances, relational risk is unavoidable.

Strategic alliances face a major risk in terms of opportunism, which can be seen as seeking gain for oneself at the expense of others. In such cases, there is a high probability of breaches to the contract. Organizations in an alliance fearing threat of opportunism are faced with a greater need to screen, negotiate, and monitor partners' behavior, thus leading to increased transaction costs.

A question to deliberate at this point is: Does opportunistic behavior hurt an organization's image, reputation, and potential for future business? Definitely. Opportunistic behavior that is oriented toward individual organization's benefit rather than to the good of the alliance leads to relational risk. Organizations, therefore, need to understand that opportunistic behavior does not pay off in the long run.

Performance Risk

Performance risk is the possibility that the alliance might fail even though the partner organizations commit themselves fully to the alliance. Despite the efforts of the partner organizations, an alliance may fail because of a number of internal and external factors. External sources for failure include environmental factors, such as change in government policies, economic recession, change in customer behavior leading to demand fluctuations, failure of a coveted technology, or fierce competition. Internal factors may include lack of competence in critical areas or complete bad luck. Unlike relational risk, performance risk is part of every strategic decision, as performance can always fall below one's expectations. Whereas relational risk comes into picture only when organizations get into an alliance, performance risk is linked to any undertaking and gets shared by all the partners. For example, joint bidding in case of risky projects helps the partner organizations to not only share the costs, but also to share the risks involved. Rather than handling projects alone, organizations get into a strategic alliance to reduce their performance risk. Taking the Tata–Starbucks joint venture, the alliance helps both the organizations to share the risk and cost of setting up coffee retail chains in the country. The alliance continues to face the risk from various external environmental factors. The probability always remains that the organizations have overestimated the shift from tea to coffee. Customers may still prefer tea over coffee. An economic recession that eats into customers' pockets would reduce footfall to the various coffee stores opened by the joint venture. Acting in an aggressive manner to fight industry competition also dents the chances of success of the alliance. Financials exhibit the performance risk, with the joint venture showing a profit after tax in negative. Joint venture partners can afford low levels of performance risk. It is difficult and costly to exit a joint venture agreement as compared to a licensing agreement.

Risks in Managing Alliance Resources

The unique resources and capabilities possessed by an organization form the core foundation of its competitive advantage in the marketplace. Managing the various resources, that is, identifying, utilizing, and protecting the critical and valuable resources, is important for business performance. In case of an alliance, resources management can be looked at through four perspectives: optimally using one's own resources, developing and enhancing those resources, protecting one's own resources so that they are not unintentionally transferred or imitated, and gaining access to the resources owned by the other organization.

When organizations work independently, they are primarily concerned with managing resources through the first three aspects. Strategic alliances put forth the possibility of gaining access to the valuable resources owned by the other organization. Strategic alliances, though, help organizations to develop their own resources and explore innovative ways of utilizing their own resources.

While alliances give access to the resources owned by the other organization, the disadvantage is that protecting one's own resources becomes a challenge. Organizations will be at a disadvantage if their resources get imitated by the partner organization or get unintentionally transferred.

Organizations, therefore, are always in a race to protect their own critical resources and at the same time attempt to make maximum use of the resources contributed by the partner organization. The type of resources that an organization brings to the alliance determines what is at stake and what risk of loss the organization faces.

Types of Primary Resources: Property and Knowledge

Organizations contribute a lot of resources to the alliance. Resources can be classified into two categories depending on their nature and the protection of law offered to them. Property resources include physical and financial resources that are explicit, tangible, and have clear property rights attached to them. Examples may include plant and equipment, a distribution network, patents, contracts, logos, trademarks, and so on. They are protected by law and cannot be freely obtained, as they have an ownership barrier. Knowledge resources are primarily the tacit resources, including technological and managerial expertise, that are not directly protected by law, but by a knowledge barrier. Organizations need to decide on the knowledge barrier so that unintended knowledge and information do not get leaked to the partner organization.

In cases of licensing agreements, researchers have referred to a *boomerang effect*, whereby the licensee of a new technology develops it to the extent wherein it ends up overtaking the licensor. It is evident that organizations that license out their technology need to protect themselves from being put out of business by the licensee organization.

For example, in the case of Tata–Starbucks joint venture, the resources being contributed to the alliance include the distribution network, an understanding of the customer behavior, the Tata and Starbucks brand name, and the managerial expertise with respect to processing and roasting of coffee beans. Managing these resources would be critical for both Tata and Starbucks.

Strategic Alliance Orientation for Managing Risks

As illustrated in Figure 5.1 management executives have multiple choices with respect to managing the risks involved in a strategic alliance.

Control

In alliances where partner organizations do not have complete trust on each other with probability of relational risk being high, and the resources involved in the alliance are property resources, management executives are advised to instill control in the alliance. Control can be managerial, equity, and contractual control. For greater managerial control, organizations try to have their executives in key positions in the alliance so that they have greater control over the decisions take. For equity control, organizations try to negotiate for a greater equity stake or ownership in the alliance. Greater equity control also implies more authority and decision

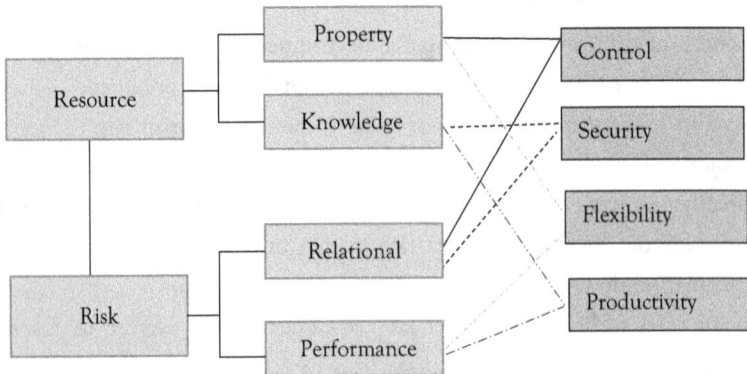

Figure 5.1 Orientation for managing risks

making. Shared ownership also aligns the interests of partner organizations and dissuades opportunistic and deceitful behavior. This control is, however, relevant only if the alliance involves an equity creation. For example, joint ventures because of the system of ownership instill financial controls. Boundaries are clearly delineated, thereby holding personnel accountable for collaborative outcomes. Participatory and shared decisionmaking can also help to inhibit opportunistic tendencies.

Because of the trust that develops between partners, joint ventures also make informal controls possible. Trust can reduce the need to form complex and costly contracts. Also, as inter-partner trust grows, organizations become inclined to expand ties and contribute their resources to the joint work of the alliance. Trust can be goodwill or competence. Whereas goodwill trust is based on one's good faith, intentions, and integrity, competence trust is the trust that partners have that the other partners will act as per the competence they have built.

Contractual control implies clear specification of terms and conditions of the alliance and clear specifications with respect to the usage of property contributed to the alliance. For example, a *grant-back* clause in the licensing agreement might require that any improvements made to the licensed technology must be shared with the licensor. Both managerial and contractual controls are applicable for all kinds of alliance agreements. Prespecified rigorous contracts are useful because they reduce the risk of defection and also facilitate legal enforcement. However, care needs to be taken as contract-based governance might also inhibit trust between partners.

A question that can be deliberated here: *Can outcome controls help to manage risk?*

Flexibility

In alliances where the risk of the alliance not performing as per the targets laid down is there, and the resources contributed to the alliance are predominantly properties, management executives are advised to keep the terms and conditions of the alliance flexible. The need of the hour is to keep a balance between contractual rigor and flexibility. Flexibility allows partner organizations not to be tied down to rigid, inflexible terms and conditions, thereby leaving scope to adjust and adapt the alliance as per the changing circumstances. Short-term contracts can be designed that give partner organizations the choice to move out of the alliance in case of failure. Another option in front of organizations is to specify clear exit terms and conditions. Partner organizations can introduce a lock-in clause that binds them for a minimum period after which the organizations are free to move their separate ways in case they desire. Such a provision enables organizations to minimize the sunk costs, adjust to new situations, and recover more investment in case the alliance fails. For example, in the alliance formed between the Future Group and Gini and Johnny, either of the two partners had the choice to move out by giving three months' prior notice, but only after completion of the initial lock-in period of two years. This clause not only added flexibility to the alliance, but also ensured that no partner acted in an opportunistic manner.

Security

This pertains to alliances where there is lack of trust on the other partner, and predominantly tacit technological and managerial knowledge is contributed to the alliance, and the likelihood of one's know-how being stolen by the partner organization is high. Management executives can make an attempt to secure such knowledge by instilling various knowledge barriers. A question that can be asked is: *Can information flows be controlled in an alliance?* Probably, yes by defining rules for employees that describe clearly what they can and cannot discuss with the partner. Steering committees set up in alliances provide the administrative apparatus to guide interactions of partners by providing a formal channel through which partnering organizations can share information and respond to the reckless behavior of managers, if any.

As mentioned previously, partner organizations in an alliance are in a race to learn, and knowledge plays an important role in today's competitive environment. A partner that manages to learn more gets a greater bargaining power.

Limiting scope of the alliance is another means of protecting knowledge leakage. Establishing the scope of activities for an R&D alliance involves decisions such as whether to restrict joint activity to precompetitive R&D

only or to extend it to include manufacturing and marketing. Another important aspect is whether the development project can be effectively modularized and conducted in isolation from other activities of the parents. It is brought together only in the final stages, in contrast with an arrangement that involves intensive cooperation and knowledge sharing throughout the project duration. Contributing competencies or bundle of skills to the venture rather, than dispersed skills or assets, reduces the probability of opportunistic behavior.

The more extensive, interdependent, complex, and uncertain are the activities performed in the alliance, the greater is the potential risk of opportunism. Greater coordination and face-to-face interaction is required in this situation. It also raises the costs of monitoring and assessing partner behavior.

When organizations look out for collaborators in technology-related projects, they should target partners whose strategic goals converge, but competitive goals diverge. If both partners target the same end-product market, then their competitive goals converge, and each would be busy in internalizing each other's knowledge and at the same time limiting access to their own proprietary knowledge. This would defeat the goal of the alliance.

Productivity

This pertains to alliances where risk of the alliance not performing is there, and the resource primarily contributed is knowledge. To deal with this kind of risk, organizations need to focus on increasing the productivity of their knowledge, that is, making an effort to ensure that the know-how is used effectively to improve results from the alliance. It is also important that the know-how of one partner is combined effectively with the know-how of the other partner. For this, it is important that partner organizations adopt each other's superior knowledge. An organizational learning climate that promotes transfer of know-how across organizational boundaries is important. This is in contrast to relational risk where critical knowledge needs to be protected to prevent opportunistic behavior. For example, in the case of Tata–Starbucks alliance, it is important that know-how of both partners, Tata's knowledge of the

Indian customers and the industry and Starbucks' knowledge of superior roasting of coffee beans is effectively leveraged to chart out a competitive space in the retail coffee industry.

Collaborating With Competitors

With industry boundaries getting blurred, a very pertinent question in front of management executives is: Who is my competitor? Executives need to be alert about existing competitors and also potential competitors. Are Tata Tea and Starbucks, or Honda and Hero Motors, competitors at the time of forming the alliance? Interestingly, GE collaborated with Samsung to develop microwave ovens. Now Samsung competes with GE in full line of household appliances.

No doubt, alliances with competitors introduce considerable risks, yet alliances among competitors are very popular. A word coined to describe collaboration with a competitor is: *coopetition.*

Drivers of Coopetition

Very few organizations have mastered the art of maintaining a balance between cooperation and conflict in coopetition, thereby intensifying the risks to be managed in an alliance. Having identified existing and potential competitors, management executives seek to understand the value of collaborating with a rival. There are various reasons why organizations are motivated to collaborate with their rivals.

Set Standards in the Industry

Organizations form alliances to set standards in the industry and alter the basis of competition. New standards introduced set fresher benchmarks for competition in the industry. When Airtel, Vodafone, and Idea collaborated for sharing of towers and the passive infrastructure, they were aware that the concept, though tried out in many developed markets, was unheard of in the Indian telecommunication industry. Sharing of towers, thereby reducing duplication of resources that was driving up the costs of operations for the telecommunication players, introduced a new standard of operating for other players in the market.

Sharing of Risks

Collaborating with competitors also enables organizations to share the risks of taking a strategic decision, be it the risk of introducing a new product or technology in the market or the risk of entering into a new market.

The alliance between Suzuki and Toyota for developing electric vehicles enables the players to share the risks of developing a new technology and also the risk of backlash from other competitors in the industry.

Enter Emerging Markets

The emerging markets having a huge potential for growth have seen an influx of foreign players entering into an alliance with Indian rivals. An alliance with Indian organizations helps the foreign players overcome the entry barrier and also learn from the customer insights of the local player. In case of industries protected by the government foreign direct investment (FDI) rules and regulations, an alliance with a local rival helps the multinational player set up a base in India. In the Tata–Starbucks joint venture, the alliance helped Starbucks to enter India and also adhere to the government regulations with respect to FDI in the retail industry.

Expand Product Lines

Organizations many times form alliances to expand their product lines and scale up operations in a new geography. Partnership between Mahindra and Mahindra and Ford India for developing a sports utility vehicle and an electric vehicle enables both the players to expand their product lines. If Ford India, through this alliance, is able to scale up its operations, India could very well serve as the hub for reaching out to other emerging markets.[2]

This alliance, however, would put Ford in direct competition with Suzuki and Toyota in the electric vehicle category. To be successful, partners need to understand the risks of coopetition and manage it accordingly.

---

[2] Ghosh, M., and A. Raj. 2018. "Ford Posts a profit in India, 20 Years After Driving It." *Live Mint* October 23, 2018 https://livemint.com /Auto/OZIyEU-Kiu91VH2APzOspjK/Ford-posts-a-profit-in-India-20-years-after-driving-in. html (accessed August 30, 2019)

Reduce Costs

Organizations form alliances to combine similar assets and thereby reduce costs. As direct competitors own similar type of assets, they make efficient partners for this purpose. The coming together of Airtel, Vodafone, and Idea to combine their towers in different circles was primarily driven to bring down costs of operations in the face of falling average revenue per user. The agreement between Ford and Mahindra and Mahindra, with the latter developing petrol engines, would help Ford India to reduce its development costs to the minimum.

Increase Market Share

Organizations often form alliances to increase market share and generate powerful network effects. The increased market share not only helps one to compete effectively against rivals, but also helps to attract suppliers and customers. This would help the players to increase the scale of operations and also to establish a network of associations. Rivals like General Motors, Daimler Chrysler, and Ford came together to increase the market share and create the scale required to succeed.

Create New Business

Alliances between rivals at times also help organizations to enter into new businesses. For example, in the joint venture between NBC and Microsoft, in the online and cable news business, NBC contributed broadcasting skills and assets, whereas Microsoft provided online and technical expertise to create skills in a new medium that merged TV and computing. The alliance helped Microsoft to further its foray into the communications business and NBC to move out of the traditional broadcasting business.

Risks of Coopetition and Managing Them

The risks discussed in the first half of the chapter get magnified when we talk about collaboration among competitors. The question before management executives is to identify some of the risks their organization face when getting into an alliance with a rival player and to explore ways of managing those risks. Organizations defaulting with respect to managing coopetitive risks will be at a competitive loss *vis-à-vis* the rival organization.

Leakage of Critical Technology

In the current technology era, technology is at the core of competitive advantage for many players. In case of coopetition, the risk of technology leakage increases, as the rival organization is in a position to make immediate use of the technology at stake.

Organizations try to manage this risk by either controlling the flow of information or by securing their technology by filing a patent for the same. Information flow can be controlled by creating rules, laying down clearly what employees can and cannot discuss with the partner. Where a critical technology is involved, management executives need to be very careful when identifying the scope of the activities in the alliance. For example, organizations owning critical technology might include all activities post technology development in the scope of the alliance. In the alliance between Eli Lilly and Ranbaxy, the research and development (R&D) activities on the drug molecules were kept by Eli Lilly outside the scope of the alliance. The manufacturing and marketing of generic drugs formed part of the alliance. In this case, Eli Lilly was apprehensive of the leakage of the core R&D expertise in case the molecule discovery activities were located in India.

Revealing the Strategic Plans and Intentions

An alliance with a competitor also implies that the organization faces the risk of exposing its strategic plans and aspirations for the future. This might tip off the rival organization to think in a similar direction that robs off the competitive edge the decision might have for the organization. The plans and intentions might get revealed explicitly during high-level talks between the management of the two organizations. But, at times, transfer might be indirect through an intimate understanding that one gets of the other partner on account of working close together with the other organization.

Management executives face a tough task here. Controlling too much information might be detrimental to building relationship with the other partner, but revealing critical information not within the scope of the alliance might be risky for the future of the organization. This risk, therefore, cannot be completely eliminated, but can be controlled through a better management of the information flows. For example, in many alliances, the senior management conveys to the managers and executives the critical nature of the information and sensitizes them to the guidelines to be followed for sharing the information. Gatekeepers deputed also inhibit direct contact with all the staff with all information getting routed to the partner through these selected gatekeepers.

Defection of Key Customers

Organizations are wary of putting their key customers in direct contact with their rival partners. The risk of the partner stealing away the customers in the near future, through better offerings and customer understanding, is imminent.

How can management executives manage this risk? There can be multiple approaches, with organizations insisting on joint interaction with the customers. Secondly, a reciprocal access to the partner's customers is another approach to collaboration. Lastly, organizations might allow access to customers only in case of sale of joint products.

For example, in the case of Honda and Hero Motors' alliance, the risk of customers defecting toward the Honda brand was great, once Honda had built awareness of its brand in India.

Slow Decision Making

Alliances with competitors are likely to lead to delayed decision making. We are talking here of two players who are trying to achieve the same strategic goal and in whom the feeling of supremacy runs predominantly. None of the partner is willing to take a step down with respect to the strategic decisions taken. Rather than the complementary synergistic relationship, the alliance has all the potential to become a contending one.

To expedite the decision-making process, it becomes very important that the partners identify their area of expertise and take onus for the strategic decisions accordingly. Alternatively, partners can focus their efforts on different points along the value chain. For example, in the alliance between Amtrex and Hitachi, Amtrex took ownership of the decisions in the area of marketing, sales, and distribution, whereas Hitachi took ownership of product development.

Sale of Interest in the Alliance at Below-Market Price

Alliances between competitors also create the risk of one of the partners being forced to sell its stake in the alliance at below-market price, that is, a fire sale. In case of coopetition, the bargaining power might tilt very easily in favor of one of the other partners, who might then be interested in the other's business rather than in cooperation. The probability of evincing interest from a third party to acquire stake in the joint venture being low, the partner with lower bargaining power is left with only one buyer, the partner, for selling its stake. Whereas the partner is able to command a price favorable for it for buying the stake in the joint venture, the outgoing partner gets benefitted by not being tied down to an alliance that might not be making any business sense for it.

An important question to deliberate is: *Do alliances involving competitors exhibit any particular pattern with respect to choice of the alliance structure?* Probably yes. Most of such alliances get established as joint ventures.

Figure 5.2 illustrates the importance of clear assessment of the risk involved in a strategic alliance.

Alliances, though, have become an important tool for organizations to achieve their objectives, but there are risks involved, and management executives need to tread with caution. The portfolio theory when applied to organizations having a portfolio of alliances exhibits that organizations need to choose partnerships, reflecting a desirable mix of return and risk.

From the preceding discussion, it is evident that organizations in an alliance face risks from various quarters, and they need to identify these risks before they negotiate the terms and conditions of the alliance. Clearly thought out terms and conditions can help organizations manage the various risks.

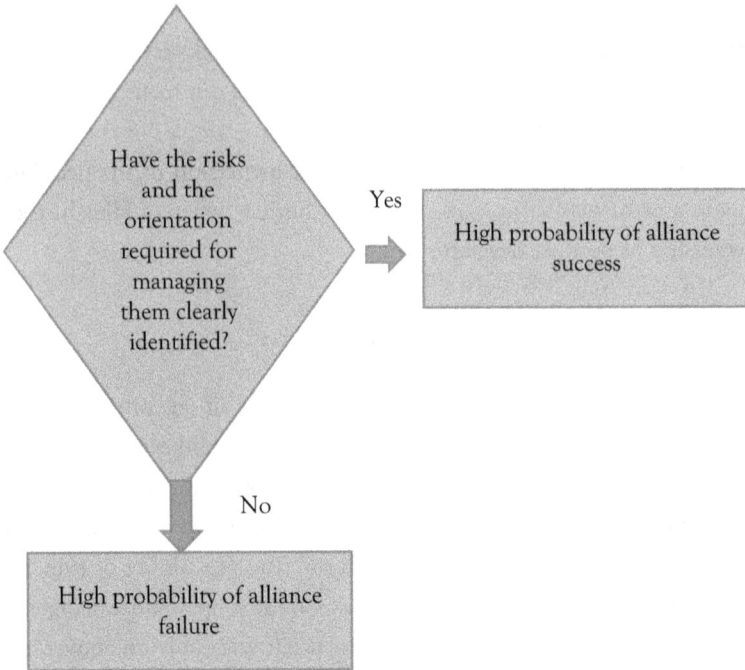

Figure 5.2 Outcomes of risk assessment and management

CHAPTER 6

Negotiating the Deal

It is rightly said that up till now, it has been a courtship period in the course of the alliance life cycle, with both the partners trying to present a very positive picture about themselves. It is at the negotiation stage when all the economic and financial matters get discussed, all the bitterness starts. Management executives need to be very careful with respect to the conduct of negotiation talks so that they do not cut a bad deal. It is important for executives to link the negotiation strategy to the nature of intended relationship. As the partners start with the process of negotiations, the dynamics that come into play may be influenced by a number of factors like perceptions of trust and relative power.

Doing Homework for Negotiations

To avoid various problems in negotiations, it is important that management executives address key issues in three areas: preparing for negotiation, building the negotiation team, and conducting the negotiations.

Preparing for Negotiations

Before entering into negotiation discussions with a potential partner, management executives need to prepare for the talks on various fronts. Most important of all, they need to decide on the overall negotiation strategy and the tone they would use during the negotiation talks. An important question they need to be clear on: What should be the focus of the talks: discussion on hard, economic facts or a focus on building amicable relationships? For example, in some countries, like India, the focus during the initial rounds of discussion is to build trust and relationship with the potential partner before hitting on the hard, economic matters. The intention might be to remove perception of any opportunistic behavior.

The executives also need to build an *alliance aims and constraints sheet*. A clarity on the objective of the alliance and any constraints to the conduct of the alliance should be clearly known. For example, an existing alliance the organization has might restrict it from operating in a particular geography or a product or technology. In subsequent alliances, executives need to be cognizant of these restrictions. An *alliance aims and constraints sheet* helps managers to focus on issues that are important for the alliance and not enter into negotiation battles over peripheral issues. An understanding of the goals and expectations of the organization from the deal, as well as the organization's understanding of the goals and expectations of the other party, is always helpful.

A roadmap or a chronology of events should be clearly laid down. For example, executives might propose a confidentiality agreement being signed in the initial meeting, followed by a memorandum of understanding or a joint venture document in subsequent meetings.

Another relevant question that executives need to mull over is: *What should be the location of the negotiation talks?* Is the location of talks important? In the Fiat and Tata alliance, during the negotiation talks that were conducted at the Tata headquarters, the Fiat executives got frustrated with the Tata executives moving in and out of the negotiation room to handle operational, day-to-day queries. Another important fact to be kept in mind is that the cost of traveling is involved in negotiation talks. Will just one partner bear the cost or partners share the cost by alternating the talk locations? In many alliance negotiation talks, neutral locations are preferred by the potential partners.

A continuing question is: *Are electronic negotiations an easy way out of the preceding debate?* Probably not, if the purpose of the meeting is to build trust and discuss critical issues.

Before going for the talks, it becomes important to identify the key relationships at play in the counterpart party and the most difficult-to-persuade player so that focus could be on him or her.

Building the Negotiation Team

Another important decision to be taken is the constitution of the negotiation team that shall conduct the talks. Who should be part of the team? It is advisable to take on board executives who either have had the experience of conducting prior negotiation talks or are good in building interpersonal skills. At times, an executive from the same nationality as that of the potential partner helps to build trust. In all probability, a negotiation team should have at least one business and one legal representative. However, a lawyer whose negotiation style is aggressive might not be good for an alliance where the partners are hoping to build a cooperative relationship.

Multinational organizations exploring options of strategic alliances with Indian organizations usually feel comfortable with a team heavy on legal representatives who could advise on the nuances of legal aspects and complexities of the Indian business rules and regulations. A couple of important questions in front of the executives leading the negotiations for the alliance is: *Should the CEO be made in charge of leading the talks?* If yes, will the team be left with a fallback option in case the negotiation talks fail? If the CEO voiced support, would there be anyone who would be willing to oppose? Is there an executive of similar status and with commensurate powers to champion the negotiation talks? Should external advisors be involved in negotiation talks? Should operational managers who will be running the alliance be part of the negotiation talks?

For example, in the case of the Renault–Nissan alliance, the negotiation talks involved the top leaders and the middle managers. Three sets of people simultaneously examined the potential benefits of the deal.

They included the two leaders of the companies Louis Schweitzer and Y. Hanawa, five lead negotiators for Renault, and four lead negotiators for Nissan. These lead negotiators represented the different functional areas, ranging from finance to legal, and corporate planning functions and the various engineers and specialists from each side.

However, care needs to be taken that either the negotiating team has the authority to make decisions regarding the negotiations or has the access to higher level executives who have the necessary authority.

Conduct of the Negotiation Talks

Alliance negotiation talks can turn out to be very complicated. Therefore, it becomes imperative for management executives to be critical of various factors during conduct of the negotiation talks. First, it is important that talks are conducted in a swift and prompt manner without too much delay in finalizing the terms and conditions. Based on practice, a general rule of thumb is that negotiation talks should ideally not take more than 10 percent of the expected lifespan of the alliance. Talks that take a disproportionate length of time to close the deal fail to create value for both partners involved. With change in the business context, the business case bringing the potential partners together might not continue to hold strong. But, executives also need to ensure that critical issues and matters have not been left unattended in the quest to close the deal.

For example, in telecom deals a year of negotiations is considered to be normal: three to six months for business negotiations, three months to prepare the legal documents, and three months to get government clearances and regulatory approvals. Management executives in certain cases face the risk of closing flawed deals; deals that are signed because everyone is not only too tired to fix the problems, but also too tired to walk away.

Second, the partners to give shape to the context for negotiation might initiate the signing of various legal documents like the nondisclosure or confidentiality agreement and the formation agreement that details the business and geographic scope of the alliance and the ownership structure. The purpose of the nondisclosure agreement is to facilitate protected disclosure of confidential or proprietary information during the process of negotiation. However, even after the signing of a nondisclosure agreement, organizations should be judicious with respect to disclosing unnecessary information. The partners might, at this stage, if they want, put restrictions on the other partner from holding parallel negotiation talks through a lockout provision.

Third, developing a joint business plan is another important agenda item for the negotiating team. A joint business plan helps the teams to establish targets for the alliance and also to map out critical operating practices for the joint venture. It helps the partners to plan out how synergy could be built between the partners and development of a corporate culture that might be very distinct from the partner organizations. For example, in the case of Renault–Nissan alliance, 21 joint study teams were formed to appraise each definite element of the operations of both companies. The study teams also gave an opportunity to the different personnel to understand the primary concerns of the organizations and their cultural practices. This exercise, they felt, was important to build trust across the organizations even before the deal was signed.

Fourth, the negotiating team also needs to be sure that no other operating unit from their organization is in negotiations with the same potential partner. It creates conflict within the organization, something that can be avoided if due care is taken to do homework to determine possibilities of past, current or prospective negotiation talks with the same potential partner. For example, IBM's *vendor information system*, wherein managers put the partner's name and IBM's contact point into the worldwide database as soon as a discussion with the partner is initiated, helped to avoid the aforementioned conflicts.

Fifth, it becomes important for executives to move beyond signing of the contract. It is important that the agreement leads to an operational alliance that creates value for both the partners.

For management executives, it is also important that they learn from the negotiation experience, insights that can be used in negotiation talks with subsequent alliance partners. They need to be aware of their style of conducting negotiation talks and also be sensitive to the style adopted by the potential partner.

A question to deliberate on: *Do cultural differences play a role in negotiation?* Probably, yes. In the alliance between Hewlett Packard and Cisco,

Cisco being a conservative organization preferred to use words like *may* and *intend to*, whereas Hewlett Packard preferred to use *shall*.

Alliance Negotiation Issues

The negotiating team needs to ensure that certain critical issues are discussed, thrashed out, and a consensus reached. It is always better to discuss and brainstorm during negotiations rather than getting held up during operations when various issues surface. Some of the critical issues can be broadly categorized as establishment and postestablishment issues.

Establishment Issues

Structure

The structure of the alliance needs to be clearly thought out. Management executives need to have a clarity on what kind of alliance-equity, nonequity, or a joint venture will serve the purpose of the alliance. Organizations might decide to go for a purely contractual alliance or might opt for a joint venture set up as a corporation or a limited liability partnership. Organizations have various choices with respect to collaborative arrangements: a consortium, joint venture, equity alliance, a contractual agreement, a franchising or a licensing agreement. More the equity an organization puts into a collaborative arrangement, combined with fewer partners that it takes on, more control it will have over the operations run under the arrangement. Nonequity arrangements generally require at least one and many times several partners.

Which is the most common type of alliance? A nonequity alliance that is based on contracts between organizations. The most frequent forms of nonequity alliances are supplier agreements, distribution agreements, and licensing or franchising agreements. These alliances, through vertical strategic alliances, connect different parts of the value chain of the industry. They usually involve sharing of explicit codified knowledge.

Choice between equity and nonequity alliances involves a study of market versus hierarchy or hierarchy versus hybrid models of governance, when looked at from the transaction cost economics perspective. Organizations might opt for a contractual alliance over an equity alliance, as a contractual alliance gives more flexibility, easy exit options, low exit costs, and quick return on investment. Some reasons why organizations might opt for an equity alliance is that equity alliances provide better protection of a large-scale investment, get stronger government support, and lead to more efficient transfer and legal protection of technology.

In high-tech R&D settings, many organizations are settling to work collaboratively in a contractual alliance with no equity stake. Partnering organizations agree to include incentives and preventive measures in the contract that inspires them to act in the best interest of each other. Successful contractual alliance cooperation, however, relied on the partners' goodwill, trust, and mutual obligation toward each other as a substitute to formal contractual safeguards. The contractual alliance could prove to be too flexible to govern, and hence, the choice of equity joint ventures saved costs of negotiation, monitoring, and enforcing contracts.

Organizations tend to prefer a joint venture entity when there are multiple facets to their relationship and they envisage a long-term continuing relationship. The biggest challenge of a joint venture is that it lacks flexibility. To instill flexibility, renegotiations are required, which are time-consuming. A good joint venture agreement would have a renegotiation clause. It is, however, advisable to keep these clauses to the minimum.

At times, past experiences of an organization also help it to zero down on a structure. For example, Nippon's experience with a not very successful joint venture prompted it to negotiate for a technical nonequity alliance with ICL, India.

At times, organizations, to avoid the legal formalities and time involved in setting up a separate legal entity, might prefer an equity alliance. For example, the Renault–Nissan alliance started as an equity alliance with both partners picking up stake in each other, when both partners realized that the legalities of setting up a joint venture was leading to differences between the two. In March 1999, the alliance agreement between the two leaders allowed Renault to buy 36.8 percent of Nissan for 5.4 billion U.S. dollars. Renault was also given the right to increase the holding to 44.4 percent from May 2001, if they desired. Nissan took a 10 percent stake in Renault. Both organizations maintained their separate identities and were run by separate management teams. Equity alliances often require larger investment, as they are based on partial ownership rather than contracts. They signal stronger commitment and allow for sharing of tacit knowledge.

Management executives also need to deliberate on: should the joint venture be set up as a company or a limited liability partnership (LLP) firm? A couple of arguments in favor and against an LLP could be:

1. An LLP needs to pay a higher taxation rate (30 percent) than a company (25 percent).
2. In case of noncompliance, penalty on an LLP is higher than on a company.
3. An LLP cannot go public for raising capital.

The arguments in favor of an LLP can be:

1. An LLP can be formed with least possible capital.
2. Cost of registering an LLP is lower than incorporating a private limited or public limited company.

Approval of the regulatory authorities is also needed before entering into a joint venture. The various issues that might come up include:

- The impact of the cooperative behavior on the relevant market and the impact on customers and market efficiency.
- The impact on competition as the joint venture leads to increase in industry output, motives being procompetitive.
- Behavioral changes induced by the joint venture, as the joint venture might force partners to communicate with each other and foster cooperation that was previously absent or weak. The joint venture may also provide better means for enforcing discipline between parents because each now has a commitment that exposes it to retaliation by the other party.

Equity Stake in Case of a Joint Venture

Negotiating about ownership stake is a critical component, and the negotiating team from each organization has an important question to answer: Should I hold a majority or a minority stake in the joint venture? When exploring opportunities and knowledge in uncharted territories, it can be argued that minority stake is advisable. Equity ownership no doubt brings in the component of bargaining power according to the resources owned by partners, but a small equity stake of less than 20 percent may signal lack of commitment, and therefore increase the probability of failure.

An equity arrangement also helps to intertwine the interests of the partners and discourages opportunistic behavior by either party. Shared equity serves as a mutual hostage for partners to retaliate and punish an opportunistic party. It is more likely that a partner that contributes the tangible resources bargains for a greater equity control, whereas a partner contributing intangible resources bargains for greater decision power.

In fact, to promote more independence and a strong performance culture within the joint venture, it is advised that an outside investor (a venture capitalist or a private equity fund) should be given a 5 to 10 percent ownership stake in the venture.

What each partner brings to the alliance and its valuation should be clearly laid down. The valuation of the contribution is commensurate to the ownership stake of the partner. A dilemma that management executives might face is: How to value intangible assets, like contacts and network with gatekeepers, that determine the fate of the alliance?

Will an uncertain business environment influence a firm's equity stake? Probably, yes. In an uncertain environment, firms might prefer a minority equity-based structure so as to maintain strategic and operational flexibility. If a foreign partner has know-how on managing market uncertainty, his or her averseness to risk will not deter him from owning a larger share in the joint venture. The more knowledge the foreign partner has with respect to marketing, human resources and service, and their application in the host country, the more ownership rights he or she is willing to assume. Moreover, the older the joint venture becomes, more comfortable the foreign partner will become of doing business in the host country and would like to increase ownership.

Governance and Control

It can be argued that structural decisions are among the most important decisions alliance partners make. The reason is that structural decisions impact almost all aspects of the alliance, including operational process, control mechanisms, and even, exit possibilities. A foreign partner who wants to take advantage of the local resources (both human and natural) is likely to give part of the control to the local partner because of their local knowledge. Foreign firms usually rely on local partners to reduce risk or overcome government restrictions. If competition is the main driving force behind entering into joint venture, the foreign partner would like to have a dominant control. If the joint venture formation is motivated by learning, the foreign partner will tend to exercise less control.

Equity stake determines a partner's representation on the board. Studies have shown that minority partners have an opportunity to influence the management of the joint venture if they are careful to appoint, as their board representatives, people with a strong grasp of the joint venture's strategic circumstances and who also have sound bargaining skills and empathy for the partner's culture.

A governance structure involves decisions with respect to equity ownership and operational control. The eventual distribution of ownership and control will be attributable to the relative bargaining power possessed by the participants who presumably originate from different cultural backgrounds and distinct institutional environments. An asymmetric governance structure is one in which there is a disparity between equity ownership and operational/strategic control. Due to government restrictions on ownership, the foreign partner might be willing to trade reduced equity ownership for increased control over variables crucial for the success of the venture. It is more likely that a partner that contributes tangible resources bargains for a greater equity control, whereas a partner contributing toward intangible resources bargains for a greater decision-making power. Day-to-day operations require management with respect to staffing, pricing, product development, market development, and so on. Operational control helps the partners to be aware of the day-to-day decisions.

In the joint venture between Honda and Hero Motors, 26_percent equity was held by both the partners. A 13-member board was formed to oversee the governance. Honda had four key appointees, including the position of joint managing director, a powerful position in Indian companies. Seven members from the local ranks took charge, with the position of managing director held by Hero Motors. Similarly, in the joint venture between Sony and Ericsson, 50 percent equity stake was held by both partners. There was a representation on the board by four directors each from Sony and Ericsson. While the president was from Sony, the executive vice president was from Ericsson. In fact, tight governance rules (opportunistic reducing behavior) run contrary to extracting the maximum value from an alliance.

Another important matter that needs to be sorted out between the partners: *Who holds the right to veto key decisions?*

It is advisable that a joint venture board should have executives outside of the partner companies to provide objectivity to partner meetings. Also, the board preferably should have a nonexecutive chairman, the position getting rotated between the partners.

The government might, at times, dictate the governance structure in international joint ventures. For example, although the government allowed 74% percent FDI in telecom, it made it mandatory that majority of directors and board members, including the chairman, managing director, and CEO, needed to be residents of India.

Scope of the Alliance

Freezing the scope of the alliance is a critical component of negotiations. The scope might be decided either with respect to value chain operations, geographical coverage, or product. The understanding of the risk in the alliance helps the negotiating team in deciding the scope of the alliance. Where the partners fear cannibalization of product or technology, they might restrict the sale of joint venture product in the geographies where the partner organization dominates.

For example, the scope of the Hero Motors and Honda alliance was clearly the sale of fuel-efficient motorbikes in India. Identifying the scope of the alliance limits the potential of conflict between the partners.

Contribution of Resources

As already understood, an alliance involves contribution of resources from both partners, based on their individual competencies and capabilities. It might include both tangible and intangible resources. The latter include commitment of managerial and technical expertise to the alliance. The alliance agreement should clearly lay down the resources contributed by each partner. In case any partner falls short of the contribution, it might lead to an instability in the alliance and a further dissolution. For example, in the joint venture between Pepsi, Voltas, and Punjab Agro Industries Corporation, it was agreed that Pepsi would be dependent on Voltas for market research as well as marketing and distribution. The venture was one of the most comprehensive deals of the U.S. company that included snack food and soft drink bottling operations, a fruit and vegetable processing plant, an agro research center, and a major export operation to generate hard currency for India.[1] Similarly, when Starbucks and PepsiCo formed an alliance, Starbucks was responsible for roasting and so on of the coffee beans, while PepsiCo was responsible for sales and distribution. Both were responsible for joint product development and marketing. Michael Conway, President Global Channel Development at Starbucks, commented:

> Our expansion throughout Latin America in 2016 enables us to deliver high-quality Starbucks coffee in a convenient ready-to-drink format to our customers where they live, work and play. PepsiCo's sales expertise and distribution network makes them the ideal company to work with to unlock the Latin American ready-to-drink market and accelerate local demand for Starbucks.[2]

---

[1] "Pepsi Unit launches venture in India" *Journal of Commerce Special*, May 23, 1990, accessed September 24, 2019, https://joc.com/maritime-news/pepsi-unit-launches-venture-india_19900523.html.

[2] Starbucks Stories and News, "Starbucks and Pepsico to Bring Starbucks RTD Beverages to Latin America." July 23, 2015, https://news.starbucks.com/news/starbucks-and-pepsico-agreement-for-rtd-beverages-in-latin-america (accessed September 26, 2019)

Valuation of Contributed Resources

Another important matter to be resolved is the divergent positions on valuation, particularly nonbased nonmarket-based contributions such as expertise and insights about market and network. Partners may agree to value the assets and resources through:

1. Discounted cash flows that value the prospective cash flows of the venture in terms of present-day value
2. Capitalization approach that measures the asset value of contributions to the alliance based on the projected net income and expected rate of return
3. Cost approach that takes into consideration the cost needed to substitute an alternative contribution that would meet the objectives of the alliance
4. Industry benchmarking that places emphasis on the past valuation of similar ventures within the same industry. This approach takes into account the competitive factors that would influence partner valuation.

Performance Clause

The alliance agreement should lay down clearly the performance milestones expected from the alliance. It brings focus to the alliance activities and also serves as an important control mechanism. An alliance, consistently, not meeting the benchmarks may lead management executives to question: Should we continue with the alliance? It also brings into question the commitment and contribution of each partner to the alliance.

Restrictions on Partners

This clause should mention clearly how being in an alliance limits or restricts the partner firms from certain activities. An understanding of the probable areas of conflict of interest would help executives in framing this clause. For example, in the alliance between Honda and Hero Motors, Honda feared that if Hero Motors sold its vehicles in the geographies where Honda predominated, it would lead to a clash between the two partners and an instability in the alliance. While in alliance, Hero Motors was stopped from exporting its products to the global markets where Honda was present. Similarly, in the case of Indus Towers, the partners were restricted from setting up their own towers in the circles where Indus Towers had its own towers. To operate in those circles, the partners had to rent towers from Indus Towers. Also, the joint venture between Xerox and Fuji prohibited Fuji from using the technology outside the venture.

In this context, an important question in front of management executives is: *Will an exclusivity clause with respect to the resources help the alliance?* An exclusivity clause restricts a partner from providing a critical resource or capability to anyone outside the alliance.

Liability on Partners

The liability of partners in case of an exigency should be discussed and clearly drafted. Management executives should lay down clearly: Will it be joint or individual liability? This becomes more pertinent in case of an alliance where one of the partners is located in a geographical territory that runs the risk of a natural calamity. In such an incident, where the operations of the joint venture suffer, say due to components or technology not reaching as per the production schedule, who bears the loss needs to a clearly laid down. Will the loss be shared by both the partners, or will it be borne by the respective partner? It might lead to a dispute if the nonaffected partner wants the joint venture to switch to a third party against the wishes of the affected partner.

Postestablishment Issues

Identifying the List of Reserved Matters

Various decisions are required to be taken in the day-to-day management of the alliance. The alliance terms and conditions might have the provision that the partner handling the task takes the decisions. An alliance should ideally also identify some reserved matters, that is matters for which approval is required from the other party. A couple of such decisions are:

- Appointment or removal of senior management or statutory auditors of the company
- Change in capital structure, creation of subsidiaries, or merger and acquisition decisions
- Large capital expenses and so on

Changes to the Contract

Like any strategic decision, decisions involving strategic alliances are dynamic and need to evolve with change in time and context. All possibilities leading to a change in the contract should be discussed. For example, a multinational entering an industry restricted by the FDI norms might be interested in taking a relook at its ownership stake once the FDI norms become more liberal. Similarly, the performance measures laid down can also form the premise for bringing about a change in the contract. A change might be proposed with respect to operations, scope, performance measures, governance, and so on. Parties should clearly discuss the change control procedure and set it out in a schedule.

Dispute Resolution

During the course of the strategic alliance, it is very normal that differences will crop up between partners. This might lead to disputes. Disputes might arise over hard financial or technical issues or soft cultural interpersonal issues. In some cases, disputes might be positive, leading to new approaches, perspectives, or techniques. In other instances, they can be highly disruptive. A dispute, if not resolved, might lead to a premature termination of the alliance. Therefore, it is very important that, at the time of negotiations, a dispute resolution mechanism is laid down. The negotiating team might propose a dispute resolution committee to be constituted that would look into all dispute-related matters. The negotiating teams might also identify a common arbitration court that would address issues that could not be resolved by the dispute resolution committee. Indian parties agree for arbitration under the Indian Arbitration Act, whereas a multinational enterprise might demand arbitration in a neutral jurisdiction, being skeptical about the fairness and efficacy of the Indian proceedings. In majority of the cases, a third-country adjudication court is identified by the partners. For example, in the alliance between Jet and Etihad, the arbitration court in London was identified to tackle adjudication matters that could not be resolved by the partners.

Termination and Share Disposal

It is said that companies, which at the time of negotiation, also discuss the terms and conditions applicable at the time of termination of the alliance are able to create more value out of the alliance. The call for termination can be made by both partners or one of the partners might like to exit from the alliance. First, the partners should reach a consensus with respect to the events that might trigger a termination. Failure to achieve the targets laid down with respect to sales, market share, or technology could be one of the reasons. Change in the government rules and regulations that allow one of the partners to operate independently could be another reason. A breach of trust might also lead to a partner wanting to terminate the alliance. Second, how the shares of the partners would be disposed and the valuation of the shares should also be clearly laid out in the contract. Here, the management executives might deliberate on: Should a lock-in period be laid down? For example, in the alliance between Future Group and Gini and Johnny, a lock-in period of two years was laid down. It bound the partners to the alliance for two years, after which they could terminate the alliance after giving a three months' notice.

Treatment of Intellectual Property

Intellectual property is one of the important resources contributed by the partners. Who would own the intellectual property after the alliance terminates is an important matter that needs to be sorted out between the partners. An intellectual property that is the output of the alliance, post-termination might be jointly owned by both the partners or might be sold by one partner to the other. Another question that management executives need to answer is: Should the company give access to the intellectual property owned by it to the partner post-termination of the alliance? What would be the royalty payment for use of the intellectual property?

Figure 6.1 illustrates the importance of discussing and sorting out various issues during the negotiation talks.

Although it is not practically possible that all issues are discussed and documented in the negotiation documents, it is advisable that majority of the issues that may lead to conflict between the partners at the time of operations should be discussed and clearly laid down. Also, care needs to be taken that negotiation talks, if not fruitful, end on an amicable tone, leaving room for the partners to explore potential partnerships in the future.

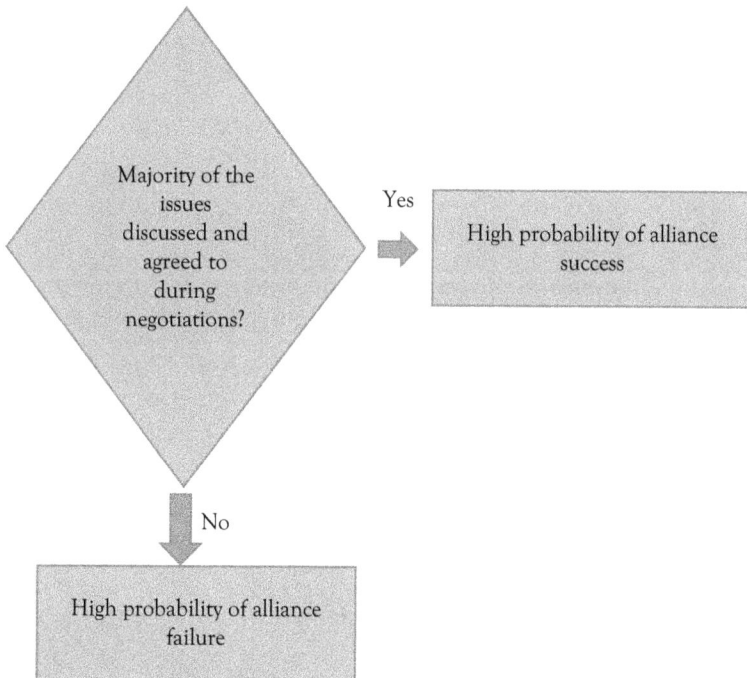

Figure 6.1 Negotiation discussion outcomes

CHAPTER 7

Managing the Alliance

After having gone through the rigor of negotiations, the partners are ready to make the alliance operational. Management executives managing the alliance, however, need to keep in mind that alliance agreement and the legal documents cannot be complete, and exhaustive that take care of all possible contingency. It is the responsibility of the managers to thrash out details in their day-to-day working with their counterparts in the partner organization. Steering committees and functional sub-committees that focus on specific activities within the alliance can serve as an administrative interface.

Managing an alliance involves managing linkages that fall in between clearly defined ones of that of a subsidiary or division of an organization to arms-length buyer–supplier relationships. The latter might have competitive elements.

A merger decision makes life simpler, only one entity needs to be managed. Joint ventures are difficult to manage, especially because they are owned by two or more parent organizations that may have competing or incongruent goals, differences in management styles, and in case of international joint ventures, additional complexities are associated with differing government policies and business practices. The broad joint venture management issues include performance, knowledge management, internationalization, cultural differences, governance and control, and valuing a joint venture. If individual interests are failed to be addressed during the launch phase, conflicts will likely develop in critical strategic areas. A couple of questions that might need deliberation include: Should the products and services of the joint venture target high-end or mass-market consumers? Should the re-investment goals of the joint venture emphasize growth in revenue or cash flow?

Managers having prior experience of managing alliances and who have internalized the learning are in a better position to manage. The joint venture management group or the steering committee is a small group of highest ranking managers of the international joint venture. This group typically includes the general manager, deputy general manager (if such a position exists), and other managers who report directly to these two positions (typically heads of functional areas). The steering committee, by being the locus of decision-making and administrative command, can improve coordination, adapt to changing conditions, and provide a platform to tackle disputes.

If a partner has access to critical technology, he or she can demand the top-most position in the venture. The partner who does not win the position bargains for other positions so as to get due representation in the joint venture. New positions (deputy GM) might also be created. Normally, functional head positions are taken by partners depending on their core capabilities.

The composition of the management team has important implications for the joint venture's performance because these managers bring their individual experiences, biases, and their parent firms' perspectives to the joint venture management team. Furthermore, the joint venture leadership team almost always includes some managers of differing nationalities and cultural backgrounds.

Challenges in Managing an Alliance

Ambiguous Alliance Relationships

Partner organizations are independent organizations with their agendas. Many times, they might be rivals coming together to form an alliance.

Partner organizations might have different motives; one can never be cent percent sure of the organization's intentions to collaborate. Managers involved in the alliance might have different expectations and commitments to their tasks. Also, alliances are conceived and negotiated at the higher levels of an organization, while the lower levels are responsible for the day-to-day management and supervision of the alliance. Managers, at times, may be faced with a dilemma with respect to the amount of transparency required in the relationship. Lastly, alliance relationships evolve with time and not necessarily in a positive direction. For example, in an alliance between a U.S. firm and a Taiwanese organization, the former trusted the partner organization for manufacture of a number of key products. The U.S. organization's managers were subsequently shocked to learn that the Taiwanese were planning to commercially exploit and compete with the Americans, the energy-saving technology that the latter had developed over the years. The failure to monitor the alliance and adjust its management practices cost the U.S. organization dearly. In an alliance, care also needs to be taken that alliance personnel deputed to the task has a high tolerance for ambiguity.

Balancing Cooperation and Competition

Strategic alliances draw a thin balance between competition and collaboration. Partners in an alliance are always in competition to learn more from the other. Even the most successful of alliances exhibit this conflict. Ford even after being in an alliance with Mazda feared to get into an alliance with the latter in European markets fearing it would turn out to be a potential competitor in the European markets. An interesting quote by a Nike executive also reflects this: "Nike has alliance with retailers. We play an active role in growing our retailers (so that they can show case Nike's brand experience. Retailers also have private labels that compete with us."

Too much suspicion of the intentions of the other partner can immobilize the relationship. Trying to draw a balance between trusting one's partner and ensuring that the strategic interests and assets of the other partner are not compromised is a difficult task. Interestingly, organizations are into a number of alliances, some of which are with rivals. Information flows into different alliances need to be critically managed.

Mindsets of Managers

Historically, most of the organizations have operated as independent entities, with the concept of alliances picking up recently. Most of the managers, therefore, are inexperienced in managing alliances. Also, managers' faith in success of alliances being low does not sound an optimistic note for the alliance. Secondly, the structure of the respective organization limits the flexibility and autonomy of individual managers.

Complex Innate Issues

Managing an alliance involves giving consideration to complex fundamental issues associated with the linkages between strategy, structure, systems, and staff in the participating organizations. It is very important for the alliance manager to see the alliance in relation to the organization's long-term strategy. A product manager selected as the alliance manager needs to see the connection between the product development alliance and the organization's long-term strategy. The product development alliance might be linked to the organization's long-term innovation strategy.

There are bound to be differences in the system-wide practices between the two organizations. These practices might vary from their incentive system to how decisions are taken within the organization. These differences compound if multiple partners are involved in an alliance. As the number of partners increase, chances of ex-post disagreements about the original aims of the contract increase. More partners also increase the transaction cost of monitoring contractual terms. How the gap and costs are bridged would determine the success of the alliance.

In international alliances, difficulties crop up not only because of differing corporate cultures, but also due to differing national cultures. Language and psychological differences might lead to gross misunderstandings among the partner organizations, thus hindering building of trust. For example, in the alliance between HP and Cisco, although both organizations had the same national culture, their corporate cultures differed, with Cisco having a conservative mindset and HP having an aggressive mindset. The alliance between IBM and Lenovo witnessed differences cropping up because of different national cultures. Whereas,

IBM's decision-making style was decentralized Lenovo's style was centralized in the top management.

Coordination Between Alliances

Another point deserving attention is the fact that organizations have a portfolio of alliances. The strategic rationale of each alliance might be different. Also, the demands placed on the resources of the organization by each alliance might be different. This creates a daunting task of maintaining a fine balance between all the alliances, not jeopardizing the future of any alliance. For example, Renault not only entered into an alliance with Nissan, but also with Chinese state-owned enterprise Dongfeng. The Renault–Nissan alliance further collaborated with the German luxury car manufacturer Daimler to develop technologies. Nissan, on the other hand, got into an alliance with Mitsubishi to develop a low-price mini car-based electric vehicle. In effect, it was a network of alliances being managed by the two companies Renault and Nissan.

The problem does not end there. Organizations are also under pressure to manage the interface between the network of internal subsidiaries and the network of alliances. Two alliances in an organization's portfolio might either complement each other or may be in conflict with each other. A good coordination among the various alliances would help the organization to enjoy the value created from multiple partnerships. A poorly managed alliance portfolio might lead to conflict among partners and waste of scarce resources, including managerial bandwidth.

As is evident from the preceding section, the task of managing an alliance is not an easy task. Until and unless there is commitment from different levels within an organization, making an alliance successful is a difficult job. It is important that the alliance committees meet regularly to monitor the progress of the alliance projects and to ensure that they receive sufficient resources and the attention from the management. The role of the corporate-level committees is to keep the various functional heads and business area heads informed of the progress on various projects.

As illustrated in Figure 7.1, the task of managing the alliance can be looked at from two perspectives: the role of the top management and the role of the alliance manager.

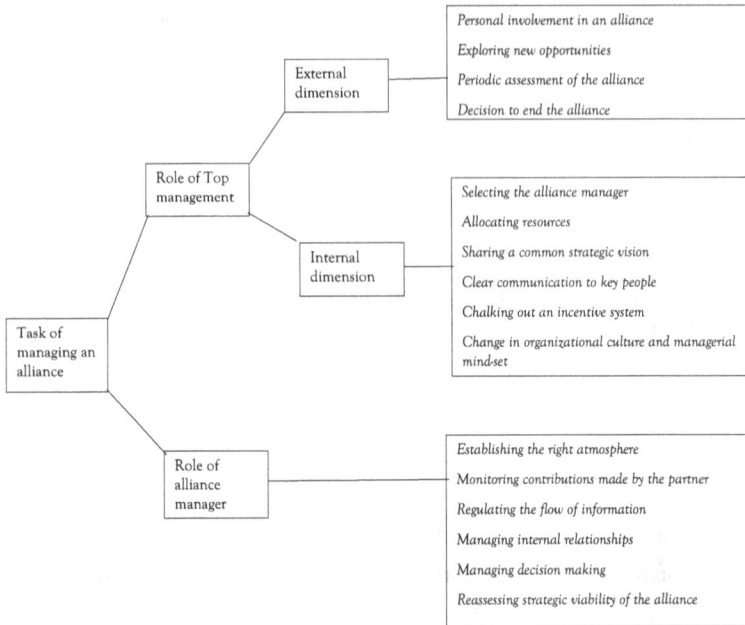

Figure 7.1 Managing an alliance

Role of the Top Management

Involvement of the top management is, in no doubt, critical for the alliance, but it is not day-to-day involvement that is expected from the top management. It is the treatment given to the alliance by the top managers that sends signals to the lower-level alliance managers and other executives in the organization. The top management's role has an external and an internal dimension.

External Dimension to Top Management's Role

The external dimension involves the relationship of the top management with the partner.

Frequent involvement by top managers in an alliance indicates to the partner that an organization attaches considerable importance to the alliance. It encourages the partner to reciprocate the relationship. For example, in the Renault–Nissan alliance, leaders from both companies were closely involved with the alliance from the inception stage. They picked up stake in each other, thereby signaling the faith companies had in collaborative working. An alliance that lacks reciprocal goodwill would lead to unresolved differences, and hence, instability in the alliance.

The role of the top management is also to get personally involved in various review meetings and discussions. Personal involvement is often equated to personal commitment of the top manager. It also encourages dedication and commitment from the lower levels. Absence of organizational commitment on the part of one or both the partners has the potential to cripple an alliance. On the other hand, close interaction at multiple levels of the partner organizations leads to a stronger alliance.

Exploring New Opportunities

The interest of the top management in the alliance also lays the ground for exploring new opportunities. Partner organizations that become comfortable of working with each other try to evaluate alternative projects where there is a possibility of an alliance. Working with existing partners is always conceived to be preferable to searching for new partners. An organization saves on the costs involved in searching for new partners, doing due diligence exercise, and then working on building trust. For example, the Fiat–Tata alliance started as a sales alliance, with Tata responsible for distribution of the Fiat cars through its showrooms. Working together made the organizations evaluate the possibility of joint production of cars at the Ranjangaon plant. Similarly, the alliance between Suzuki Motor Corporation and Toyota Motor Corporation to share product portfolio led to the companies exploring the possibility of drawing synergies by sharing infrastructure and dealer networks.[1]

Periodic Assessment of the Alliance

The controls and discipline that drive partner organizations to periodically assess an alliance comes from the top. In every strategic review, it becomes imperative not only to take stock of the performance of the alliance in terms of performance metrics established, but also to question the utility and the effectiveness of the alliance. Although it is the task of the alliance manager to assess the alliance on a day-to-day basis, the role of the top

---

[1] ET Bureau. 2019. "Inside Maruti's and Toyota's Plan to Completely Dominate India's Auto Market." May 28, 2018 https://economictimes.indiatimes.com/passenger-vehicle/toyota-maruti-suzuki-to-share-factories-dealers-for-bigger-india-footprint/articleshow/64327070.cms (accessed September 22, 2019).

management lies in assessing the alliance in context of the overall strategy of the organization. Additionally, it makes the lower-level managers accountable for briefing the top management with respect to the alliance performance. The strategic review entailed the lower-level managers to delve into multiple aspects of the alliance, which could have the potential of evolving into a strategic review opportunity for the entire organization. It also provides an occasion to the executives to learn in depth about the relationship with the partner and the extent of involvement of the different employees in the alliance. The review meetings between executives also help organizations to learn from each other's perspective.

Decision to End the Alliance

As an outcome of the alliance review process, the outcome might be the need to end the alliance. Here, the role of the top management is very important. It the ultimate responsibility of the top management to decide when and how the alliance needs to be terminated. It is the top management who is able to assess the utility of the alliance with respect to the changing strategic priorities of the organization. Close interaction of the top management with the partner also helps to assess the importance to the alliance given by the partner. Such an input is critical for the timing and manner of ending the alliance. It is also important for the top management to decide the way in which the alliance ends: on cordial terms or in an acrimonious manner. It is advisable that the alliance ends in a manner that leaves potential for future alliances between the partners.

Internal Dimension to Top Management's Role

The internal dimension to the top management's role involves the message that the top managers give to the employees within the organization with respect to the importance of the alliance for the organization.

Selecting the Alliance Manager

The first important task is with respect to the selection of the alliance manager. The alliance manager plays a critical role with respect to managing the day-to-day operations of the alliance and in maintaining day-to-day relationship with the partner. The selection of an alliance manager with the skills requisite for the alliance and allocation of powers in the alliance manager to steer the alliance forward rests with the top management. A careful selection of the alliance manager gives signals to the internal managers as well as the partner the importance of the alliance for the top management. For example, after signing the alliance agreement, Louis Schweitzer of Renault asked Carlos Ghosn to go to Japan to turnaround Nissan. Having full faith in Carlos's capability, he was officially appointed as the Chief Operating Officer of Nissan. As the champion heading the alliance, Carlos was later made the Chief Executive Officer of both Renault and Nissan.

It is also important that the top management of parent organizations empower the CEOs of joint ventures to operate as its true general manager. Often, CEOs of joint ventures lack the authority to run them. Continuity is another important aspect when selecting an alliance manager. Frequent turnover in the management can lead to instability in the alliance and can be a major barrier to the establishment of interpersonal relationships.

Allocating Resources

Alliances can demand a substantial allocation of resources. It is the responsibility of the top management to decide on the amount of resource allocation for the alliance. This decision, too, sends powerful signals. Example in the Renault–Nissan alliance, the critical resource was the managerial expertise that would successfully drive cost cutting at Nissan. When the alliance began, Renault sent 20 (and later 15) executives to Japan to support widespread operational changes and to transfer knowledge from Renault to Nissan.

Also, continuous staffing and training of alliance members are very important for effective management of the alliance. It becomes important to impress on certain behavioral norms on the alliance staff and nurture desired skills.

Sharing a Common Strategic Vision

For an alliance to work well, it is essential that partner organizations share a common strategic vision. Organizations, at times, issue joint vision statements to guide their actions. A shared strategic intent leads to a common understanding of the roles and responsibilities of each partner and the scope of the alliance with respect to the overall competitive strategy of the organization. Shaping the strategic intent and communicating the same is a critical role of the top management. It is not right to assume that the strategic rationale would be understood by all the relevant people in the organization. Identification of the relevant people might vary from one alliance to the other. For example, in an R&D alliance, it would be important that not only the R&D personnel, but also the design and the manufacturing people were informed about the alliance.

Clear Communication to Key People

Communication not only helps the employees get a clear understanding of the importance of the alliance for an organization's strategy, but also the risks involved in the alliance. Employees might be required to take various steps to overcome the various risks involved. For example, in one of the alliances, the top management made no effort with respect to communicating with its executives the importance of the alliance or their roles and responsibilities with respect to participating in the alliance. The executives were totally confused with respect to the expectation the top management had from them, ultimately leading to they not contributing to the alliance. The alliance ended with it not creating value for either of the two partners.

Employees might also have a lot of fears and concerns with respect to transfer of their jobs to the partner organizations or the loss of valuable skills and experience. They might have legitimate concerns with respect to creating competitors. It is the job of the top management to lay at rest the insecurities of their managers, validate their doubts, and explain the whole picture to them.

Chalking Out an Incentive System

The task of managing an alliance is not simple. It places huge demand on the alliance managers who not only have to fall in line with the restructuring decision of the organization, but also have to meet the demands of the new job. A question is: *How to keep them motivated to perform the job as per expectations?* One of the ways is chalking out an incentive system that duly recognizes their effort. However, this is easier said than done. The incentive and reward systems are deeply ingrained in the fabric of the organization and have been built over the years. Making ad-hoc changes might not be possible. Also, in an organization, there exist different kinds of alliances. Should different incentive systems be devised for each? Alliance management might require bringing about behavioral and attitudinal changes. Should incentives be attached to these changes? Also, different alliances might require a different degree of behavioral changes. Differences between different nationalities bring in complications. For example, in an alliance between an American and Japanese organization, not only are there differences in language and culture, but also in the behaviors of the respective executives. The American executives are much more individualistic with respect to their approach as compared to the Japanese who strongly believe in collectivism. A pertinent question is: How to reward or incentivize the efforts made by an executive to bridge these gaps?

Although very difficult to come out with a concrete solution, organizations are making tentative advances toward evolving such an incentive system. Organizations employ an annual appraisal system to assess how effectively executives are managing their alliances. Although quantification of many criteria is not possible organizations are increasingly making an effort to identify and reward appropriately those behavioral characteristics that are instrumental to successful implementation of alliances.

Change in Organizational Culture and Managerial Mindset

One of the reasons why international alliances are difficult to manage is the cultural differences between the alliance partners. This also has an impact on the performance of the alliance. Differences in organizational culture have a greater impact on the performance of an alliance than differences in national and host country culture. Alliances require a change in the mindset and culture within the organization. From a mindset of self-reliance and independent working, it requires a change toward recognizing the importance of reliance, collaboration, and sharing of controls. Personal involvement of the top management in alliances, encouraging organizational commitment, conducting strategic reviews, reworking on the reward systems are all efforts toward changing the organizational culture to accommodate alliances. Research by Yoshino and Rangan, 1995, suggests that there are three areas that require the attention of the top management with respect to bringing about a cultural change: the us-versus-them attitude with respect to cooperation at all levels in the organization; the not invented here syndrome with respect to reluctance to learn and adopt practices or know-how from the partner organization; and the inability to strike a strategic balance between cooperation and competition.

An international joint venture engages three distinct organizations with distinct identity. The new organization formed can take on the characteristics of one of its parent organizations or create a unique culture that brings together elements of both the parents culture. In cases of cultural diversity, management executives can aim for cultural synergy, which is a systematic problem-solving approach toward blending diverse cultures.

Role of the Alliance Manager

For all practical and operational purposes, the alliance manager is chosen from the middle-level management positions. The middle-level management positions serve as an interface between the operational managers and the top-level management position. The middle-level managers not only understand the strategic vision of the organization and the top management but also have connect with the operational-level managers and understand the operational challenges. Alliance managers are identified from both the companies and are represented on the joint venture board so that they represent the interest of not only the parent company, but also of the joint venture.

If the alliance is closely related to the business strategy of the organization, the manager must not only have a clear understanding of the strategy, but also have a voice in formulation and implementation. He or she must have a knowledge of the resources, extensive personal networks, and a credibility with managers at all levels. For example, in the alliance between Motorola and Toshiba, the corporate vice president who had been head of the microprocessor group was designated as the alliance manager. The alliance manager is expected to manage the interdependencies among various partners, customers, and business units.

The job description of an alliance manager is ambiguous. He or she has to deal with routine issues to strategic issues. That is, his or her thinking involves immediate to long-term issues. As an alliance manager, management executives have a couple of critical tasks to perform.

Establishing the Right Atmosphere

As an alliance manager, the core task is to establish the appropriate atmosphere of trust and faith in the alliance. Building personal relationships with the partner organizations helps to set the right tone for collaborative working. Interpersonal trust discourages any kind of opportunistic behavior between organizations and also helps to improve organizational performance by reducing negotiation costs and conflicts. Trust also helps partners to develop and use joint metrics. An absence of trust might lead to suspecting the intentions of the partner organizations, thus putting at risk the continuity of the alliance.

Bridging language differences, especially in the case of international alliances, helps to reduce the complexity in the relationships. In the Renault–Nissan alliance, English was chosen as the common language, with courses being offered in English language to both Renault and Nissan employees. Carlos Ghosn himself took Japanese courses so that he could converse with his Japanese counterpart.

As an alliance manager, one's role is also to be aware of the strategy and culture of the partner organization. For example, in an alliance with a Japanese company, it is important for the alliance manager of the other organization to be sensitive to the fact that in the Japanese culture, it is considered to be rude to be late for a business meeting. Numbers and colors have different connotations in different cultures, with a particular number or color representing good luck in one culture and bad luck in another culture. In the alliance between IBM and Lenovo, the alliance was troubled with cultural clashes. In China, the decision-making power is more centralized to the top management, whereas in the United States, employees are eager to have their voice heard. As one executive said, "Americans like to talk, Chinese people like to listen."

Companies might also be rigid with respect to preserving their own working methods. Disagreements and escalating tensions might lead to breakdown in communication, further leading to delays in decision-making.

An alliance manager is accountable to the top management to show tangible results from the alliance, be it increased market share, increased sales, reduced cost, increased efficiency, and so on. Tangible results also signify commitment of both the partners and help to build trust.

Also, as an alliance manager, an effort should be to maintain continuity in the alliance team to instill trust and confidence in the partner organization. Frequent changes in the alliance team lead to disruptions that spoil the tone set for the alliance. Although it might be a difficult task for the alliance manager to hold on to the complete team during the entire span of the alliance, effort should be made to retain the core members of the team.

Monitoring Contributions Made by the Partner

The stability of an alliance is dependent on the continued commitment and contribution of human, capital, and material resources by the partners to the alliance in a timely manner. An alliance manager should keep track of the contributions, and in case of unsatisfactory contribution, should bring it to the notice of the top management. The nature and quantity of resources contributed should be adjusted to the changing strategies and goals of the alliance. From this follows that the mission and scope of the alliance need to be closely monitored.

Monitoring intellectual contributions is an important task. Intellectual contributions could be in the form of explicit documents or tacit contribution based on the skills and expertise of individuals. Here, it becomes important to ensure that executives having the requisite expertise, credentials, skillsets, working style, and personality join the alliance team. Organizations have a natural inclination to preserve their best talent for their internal projects.

To do a good job at monitoring, the alliance manager needs to clearly identify what is to be monitored. Breaking down into distinct elements and measuring those elements might be helpful. There is also a need to monitor and measure continuously. For this purpose, the periodicity needs to be established. For example, whereas sales and profits might be monitored quarterly, operational efficiencies might be required to be measured on a more frequent basis. Involving multiple people in the day-to-day observations and using both formal and informal approaches to monitoring is advisable. For example, in the HP–Cisco alliance, *joint rules of engagement* were laid down by the alliance team so that the alliance was not dependent on any one individual.

Regulating the Flow of Information

Information is present across the length and breadth of every organization. How information is captured, retained, and used within an organization also forms the crux of organizational learning. Information in an organization can be a source of competitive advantage.

Strategic alliances involve the exchange of information among partners and leveraging it to create value for the alliance. This information might be explicit and codified in the form of training manuals, documents, books, and so on, or might be tacit resting in the minds of executives involved in the alliance. It has been noticed that most knowledge exchange takes place after a certain amount of trust is built. It is the job of the manager to ensure that adequate trust is built between the partners. For example, in the case of an alliance involving transfer of technology between partners, all manuals with respect to the specifications and use of technology need to be handed over to the partner organization. Additionally, trainings conducted also help to transmit useful tacit information.

In a strategic alliance, access to a production plant or an approach used by a partner organization to solve a business problem can be an important source of critical tacit information. As an alliance manager, an important question that needs to be handled: Should executives from the partner organization be given access to the organization's production plant? Partners can learn a lot by observing each other.

Decisions are based on available information. As an alliance manager, there is a need to ensure that timely information is available to the executives. Whether or not to allow decentralized information flows is another important decision that has to be taken by the alliance manager.

As mentioned in one of the previous chapters discussing managing risks in an alliance, leakage of critical information can pose to be a major risk for the alliance and for individual organizations. Information critical for an organization's competitive advantage needs to be controlled and protected. Partners in an alliance are always in a race to grab opportunities to learn from each other. As alliances bring together partner organizations that are actual or potential rivals, alliance managers need to draw a balance between free flow of information that ensures the zest in the alliance and unregulated information that might put at risk the competitiveness of partners.

Channeling information flows through a designated officer helps to control information. The designated officer transmits collected information only after rigorous screening of the same. This ensures consistency in the information that is transmitted to the partner organization. However, centralization of information might have its drawbacks. Alliances involving intense interactions and meetings among executives from different functional areas might not be able to control the information without hampering the effectiveness of collaborative working. A reciprocal approach to controlled information flow from the partner organization might lead to information flows from both sides drying up.

Decentralized information flows, on the other hand, lead to free flow of information among the alliance executives. It leads to direct and timely interaction between managers and engineers, speeding up the resolution of alliance-related matters. A brainstorming session with the various functional heads would help a manager understand the criticality of different information. In fact, the job of the alliance manager in this case is to frequently meet the key managers and employees involved in the alliance, especially before review meetings, discuss the objectives of the meeting and come to a consensus with respect to the information that can be shared. Ways to fend off partner requests for sharing of sensitive information without appearing to be secretive should be discussed.

Having a clarity on whether the information is publicly available or not and whether the information would help a competitor could serve as a guide with respect to the information to be shared. For example, if information is publicly available and does not help a competitor, it can be freely shared with the alliance partner. But, in case the information is not publicly available and there is a risk of the information benefitting a competitor, it becomes essential to consult other managers before sharing such information with the alliance partner. Uncontrolled show of information might benefit the alliance partner. For example, in the alliance between General Motors and Toyota, Toyota engineers were able to gather information from their U.S. counterparts and learn in a swifter manner the nuances of operating in the U.S. market. With the increasing trend of smaller cars, Toyota turned out to be a potent competitor of General Motors in the U.S. market.

Maintaining detailed records of the meetings and discussions with the partner organization is advisable. It not only instills discipline, but also provides rich information for review.

In some circumstances, increased communication at lower levels may be more efficient and effective. But, in case of an alliance with large number of partners, more communication could also lead to misinterpretation, especially if different cultures are involved.

Managing Internal Relationships

In addition to maintaining relationships with the partner organization, the job of the alliance manager is also to manage relationships within the organization, across various levels. He or she needs to manage the alliance team that assists him or her in the effective execution of the alliance. For an efficient alliance, it is important for employees across various functions to actively participate. The job of the alliance manager would be extremely tedious if departmental and functional heads refuse to cooperate with him or her. Maintaining relationships with them and garnering their support would be key to the success of the alliance. There would be instances where the business unit heads were expected to do something that would benefit the whole organization, but did not benefit or was even detrimental to a particular business unit. In the HP–Cisco alliance, the alliance team thought of themselves as company middleware that spanned horizontally across the business units and vertically between the top management and the salesforce.

Getting the cooperation from middle-level managers is crucial for the alliance. The kind of networks and relationships that the alliance manager is able to maintain with them and involve them in the alliance tasks and responsibilities is important. It is also important to convince the middle-level managers about the importance of the alliance, failing which, the managers might treat the alliance more as an intrusion into their turfs. For example, in the Renault–Nissan alliance, cross-company teams and cross-functional teams were set up. In total, 11 cross-company teams were organized around *synergy* areas like manufacturing, purchasing, product platforms, and technology. Each team had 10 members, exclusively from the middle management ranks. The cross-functional teams complemented the cross-company teams.

Many times, managers make unrealistic demands on partner organizations. It is important for the alliance manager to control the expectations of the managers and also ensure that excessive demands are not made on the partner organization. Prioritizing different projects under the alliance is advisable.

Managing Decision-Making

Another important area that might lead to unnecessary confusion is the decision-making protocol within the alliance. The governance structure decided for the alliance sets the broad framework for operational governance and control for the alliance manager. At times, there might be a need felt to have a governance structure for the joint venture organization that is very different from that of the parent organizations. For instance, in case of Indus Towers, a board member donned two hats, one that of a customer and other that of a board member. Need was felt to create a governance structure where the operational issues could be disassociated from issues involving strategy- and product-level discussions.

But, too much of rigidity in the structure might rob the alliance manager from all rights in decision-making. Also, the more extensive the use of formal controls, the slower is the development of trust. This might lead to delays in decision-making, frustrate the partner organization, and hamper the smooth working of the alliance. The alliance manager should be in a position to negotiate with the top management a certain amount of autonomy in decision-making. Certain decisions that would not involve the approval of the top management need to be identified.

This would lead to quick decision-making critical to the seamless functioning of the alliance.

Decentralized decision-making not only expedites decision-making, but also motivates alliance executives to take ownership for the decisions taken by them. This helps to increase commitment within the alliance.

In case the alliance has a dominant partner, the venture gets managed entirely by the dominant partner. In case of a shared control, both partners exercise a high degree of influence over the full range of decisions of the venture. Parents tend to place their delegates into as many managerial positions. Lastly, in a split control, both parties are involved in the management of the joint venture, but they agree to control distinct functional areas based on their respective expertise levels. For example, in the joint venture between Amtrex and Hitachi, verticals of marketing, finance and HR were with Amtrex, whereas product development, design, and quality were with Hitachi. The representation on the board was likewise, three directors each from both companies.

Do cultural differences lead to differences in style of decision-making? Probably, yes. For example, it is very difficult to hurry Japanese into decision-making which un-nerves the British who are used to responding to the top management at only a few hours' notice. Japanese prefer to consult all groups before approving any design, and do not encourage changes later in the process. Americans tend to call meetings to solve problems, while Japanese tend to talk to a person in private before meetings take place.

Reassessing Strategic Viability of the Alliance

The alliance manager plays a key role in assessing the continued value being created by the alliance and in giving the feedback to the top management. The case for a business alliance rests on the interface between certain internal organizational capabilities and external environmental factors. The dynamic competitive environment requires continual reassessing of organization's strategy. The alliance manager needs to be alert to changes in the factors that might influence the stability and the continuity of the alliance. For example, an alliance formed between a multinational organization and an Indian organization in India because of the

Sources of power of the alliance manager	
Sources of positional power	
Formal authority	Position in hierarchy and the allocated responsibilities
Relevance	Relationship between task and the objectives of the organization
Centrality	Position held in key networks within and outside organization
Autonomy	Amount of discretion in a position
Visibility	Degree to which performance can be seen by others
Sources of personal power	
Expertise	Knowledge and skills relevant to the role
Track record	Relevant Experience
Attractiveness	Attributes that others find appealing and are able to identify with
Effort	Time and energy spent in performing the role

Figure 7.2 Sources of power of an alliance manager

Source: Adapted from L.A. Hill, What it really means to manage: Exercising power and influence, HBS No. 9-400-041

government regulations limiting foreign direct investment (FDI) would be impacted by the government's decision to change the FDI threshold. For instance, in the telecommunication industry, when the government increased the FDI limit from 51 to 74 percent, the multinational organizations had the choice to renegotiate for an increase in stake in the joint ventures. The alliance manager, based on the understanding of the internal capabilities of the Indian organization and the dependence on the multinational for the financial resources, is in a position to give inputs to the top management whether to heed to the demand of the multinational for an increased stake. Although the final decision with respect to assessment of strategic alliance rests with the top management, the alliance manager because of his proximity to day-to-day affairs of inter-organizational relationships is in a better position to spot changes in the partner organization in a timely manner.

An important question that needs to be answered is: *What gives power to the alliance manager?* Figure 7.2 illustrates the sources of power of an alliance manager

How to Make Alliances Work?

Trust and inter-organizational relationships are of paramount importance for making an alliance work. It is important for partners in an alliance to make relation-specific investments, establish knowledge-sharing routines, and build inter-organization trust. To accomplish an effective alliance management, it is very important to establish an effective alliance governance mechanism that ensures coordination among the various elements.

We can conclude that alliance management is a tricky and complex task involving consideration of complex systemic issues related to strategy, structure, systems, and staff in the partner organizations. Legal contracts cannot run the day-to-day business of the alliance. It cannot be left on trial and error; an alliance has to be actively planned and executed. Figure 7.3 illustrates the importance of planning and managing an alliance. It is the responsibility of alliance management to convert the contract on a piece of paper into a productive relationship. Certain companies establish forums and networks of alliance managers to facilitate sharing of alliance experience and knowledge among them. Sharing of experience and dialogues encourage and facilitate creation of *insights and ideas* to manage future alliance situations.

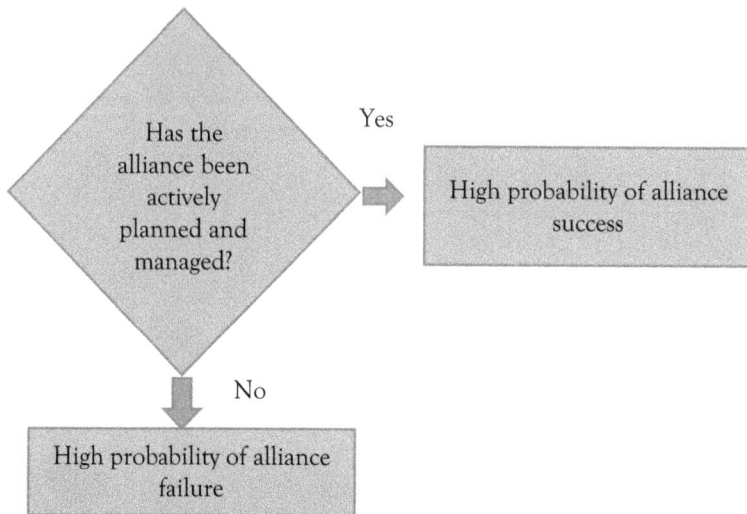

Figure 7.3 Alliance management outcomes

CHAPTER 8

Assessing the Alliance

There is a need to run each alliance as a business, with clear targets laid down. The only difference is that performance is to be measured from the perspective of both the partners. An audit is done on a regular basis, varying from 6 months to 12 months to 18 months, depending on the nature of the alliance. The audit meetings are attended by the joint venture CEO, joint venture CFO, and other top management personnel to assess the performance of the alliance. They make presentations to the board on the business, financial, and operational affairs of the organization. For example, Cisco's governance structure in most of its alliances warranted that the governing body, consisting of five to six people, met at least four times a year. The typical agenda for most of the meetings would be to assess the performance of the alliance, review the pipeline, and to resolve issues if any. In the HP–Cisco alliance, the CEOs were part of review meetings once a year.

An alliance has milestones, short and long term. Investments are made based on the milestones. Longevity of an alliance depends on how the alliance progresses with respect to the milestones. Setting performance metrics is an essential part of the alliance, and performance of an alliance is assessed based on it. As a senior executive and board member of a joint venture organization said, "Investment into the alliance is based on the various milestones achieved and longevity of a joint venture depends on how you progress on the various milestones."

The performance of the alliance can be done on the basis of any one or a combination of measures established. The measures can be set in terms of economic, strategic, operational, learning, and relational. When trying to measure economic value added by the alliance costs, revenues, profits, and return on investment serve as good indicators, whereas market share, business opportunities, competitive position, and risk reduction serve as good indicators for measuring the strategic value added by the alliance. Operational value from an alliance can be judged through measures like operational efficiency, production times, product quality, customer retention, and satisfaction. Learning outcomes and processes can be measured through indicators like gain in managerial and marketing insights, increased technological and product know-how, and exchange of explicit and tacit knowledge. Relational value added through the alliance can be measured through indicators like trust, commitment, harmony, and integrity established with the partner; the probability of opportunistic behavior; and the flexibility enjoyed in the alliance. For example, the alliance performance between Schneider Electric and Tricolite in India was assessed on the following key metrics:

- Total revenue generated
- Total columns sold
- Customer satisfaction index
- New customers developed
- Number of trainings conducted
- Number of marketing events conducted.

Based on the preceding parameters, the alliance audit committee has multiple choices:

- To grow the alliance without changing the terms and conditions of the alliance

- Fix the terms and conditions of the alliance
- Exit from the alliance

While assessing the alliance, it is important to act quickly so that set-backs can be managed. For example, Starbucks and PepsiCo were forced to rethink the direction of their joint venture after their first product carbonated coffee drink received mixed results. As one of the executives quoted, "We had a great partner, a leveraged organizational model, but no product." The partners redefined the product of the joint venture.

An important question for management executives to ponder is: *Are environmental factors crucial for stability of an alliance?* In emerging markets, government rules and regulations play an important role in deciding the stability and longevity of an alliance. Any change in the FDI limits or any change in the governance structure proposed by the government might drive the companies to reassesses the terms and conditions of the alliance, thus leading to instability. The government's decision to permit 100 percent FDI in the telecom sector against the earlier laid down 74 percent, prompted the Singtel group in 2013 to approach the Foreign Investment Promotion Board (FIPB) for buying the stake of Bharti Enterprises and Leela Lace Software Solutions (Leela) in its international and national long-distance joint venture, SingTel Global. It was expected that the government's move to increase the FDI limit would lead to more foreign organizations making an effort to increase their stake in the alliance.

The desired degree of localization and the increased insights into the market might again drive multinational organizations to reassess the value derived from the alliance and to reconsider the terms and conditions of the alliance.

The changed circumstances might lead organizations to renegotiate so as to fix the terms and conditions of the alliance. Fixing the alliance may be in terms of the scope of the alliance, the structure and equity stake in the alliance, the governance mechanism, the operations or the management of the alliance. Interdependence on each other also drives organizations to fix the alliance. Interdependence might be due to the unique resources contributed by the partners or due to the contractual terms that bind them together. Partner organizations evaluate how immediate the impact of the termination would be and the effect of the termination on its competitiveness and strategic position before taking the decision.

In case the alliance is considering major changes in the scope, structure, or management of the alliance, it is advisable that the core team comes from outside the venture. Diagnosing the performance of the venture and framing a set of options should not take more than two to three months.

Exit From Alliances

When alliances do not pay off, the working relationships among the partners can become strained, leading to bitter communication, further leading to achieving business objectives a challenge. Organizations need to plan adequately for exit from alliances. In fact, it is said that organizations that manage exit from alliances as prudently as entry into alliances are able to create more value from the alliance. What are some of the questions that management executives need to consider while planning for the exit? It is important for executives to identify the various circumstances that will trigger the dissolution of the alliance. A clarity on the impact the exit would have on the alliance portfolio is also helpful. A clear communication strategy with respect to the exit from the alliance for external and internal stakeholders should be carefully designed. Research has shown that roughly 50 percent of the joint ventures fail to meet the financial and strategic goals of the corporate parents, while 46 percent of joint venture announcements have a negative impact on the share price of the parents. Alliance managers have reported that 57 percent of their alliances fail to achieve their objectives.[1]

Exit from an alliance, especially a joint venture, is costly. Organizations in all probability try to sort out differences that crop up between it and the partner organization and resolve the deadlock when they see that some value remains from the business. Organizations are less likely

---

[1] Weiss, J., S. Keen, and S. Kliman. 2006. "Managing Alliances for Business Results : Lessons Learned from Leading Companies.",https://conservationgateway.org /ConservationPlanning/partnering/cpc/Documents /Managing_Alliances_for_Business_Results.pdf, Vantage Partners :

to exit if huge sunk costs are involved in the alliance, that is, exit and switching costs are huge. Alliance assets may be *wasting assets*, which lose their value outside the alliance. Where no consensus whatsoever can be reached between the partner organizations and partners see no value from the business the alliance is terminated, one or both the partners have the option to exercise their right to call for the termination of the alliance. Management executives here need to have a clarity on when to end an alliance. It has been found out that around 64 percent of the alliances fail because of poor and damaged relationships between the partner organizations.

Exit provisions in organizations will generally seek to accomplish one or more of the following objectives:

- Permit liquidity
- Anticipate and avoid deadlocks among partners
- Deter or punish breaches to the governing agreement

Well-thought-out exit provisions:

- Avoid triggers that require premature termination of the business, that is, before its full value could have been realized.
- Avoid triggers that would damage or discourage the business.
- Match appropriate exit right (e.g., initiating the buy or sell process or ability to force a sale) with the triggering event.
- Effect an outcome that is cost-effective and maximizes the value of the enterprise.

Permitting transfers after a minimum period ensures that partners are not locked indefinitely into an investment. Venture agreements, in case there is a default, state that the nondefaulting partners may force the defaulting members to purchase the interests held by the nondefaulting partner.

Alliances may get terminated for intended or unintended reasons. Intended terminations are planned out terminations that are governed by the end of the alliance period or the attainment of the alliance objectives. Unintended terminations are triggered due to unforeseen circumstances or unanticipated contingencies such as a breach of contract, sudden change in government rules and regulations, or a change in the status of one of the partner organizations. What is the divide between intended and unintended terminations? Approximately 90 percent of all international joint venture terminations are unintended, with only 10 percent being intended. Likewise, terminations might be friendly or unfriendly and mutually agreed upon or disputed.

Termination of joint ventures is contingent on their formation. International joint ventures that are formed for the purpose of getting access to labor, capital, and markets are less likely to be terminated for intended reasons, because the reasons for maintaining their operations are sustained unless the host country loses the comparative advantages of its country-specific assets. This rarely occurs over a short period of time. Alliances that are formed to get access to strategic assets, that are limited in supply, have more probability of intended termination as the foreign organization acquires the strategic asset.

Factors Driving Alliance Termination

Exit rights of partners in an alliance may be triggered due to a couple of reasons that might bring about a change in the business and the way it is conducted. There are various factors that might drive the termination of the alliance:

Failure to Develop the Anticipated Technology or Product

Companies, especially in a R&D or a technology alliance come together to develop a new technology. An alliance helps them to share the costs and risks involved in technology development. The nature of the alliance demands performance measures set up in terms of the development of the technology. Failure to develop the technology or nonacceptance of the developed technology by the market may destroy the value the partners gain through collaborative working. In this case, one or both the partners would like to get out of the alliance. For example, Renault and Mahindra and Mahindra got into an alliance to manufacture Logan, a car that failed to gain the anticipated acceptance from customers and the market. Also, due to the prevailing policies of the government at that time, the plan of the partners to introduce a car in India that would cost INR 7,000 never took off.[2]

Inadequate Preplanning of the Alliance

As is evident from the previous chapters, the decision to enter into an alliance is not a random decision. It requires proper planning and deliberation. Partners that get into an alliance through tactical moves, without thinking in-depth on various issues, may face challenges at various stages of the alliance. In such a case, the alliance destroys value for both the partners, thereby forcing them to terminate the alliance.

Failure to Reach to an Agreement on Alternative Approaches to Solving the Basic Objective of the Joint Venture

An alliance strategy, similar to any other strategy, evolves with change in internal and external environmental factors. The original objectives for which the partners entered into an alliance might not hold relevance, or their primary approach to reaching the objective might become redundant. In this case, it becomes important for the partner firms to explore alternative ways of achieving the alliance objectives. It is also important for them to reach to a consensus with respect to the alternative approaches. For example, Renault–Nissan together wanted to fight competition in the automobile industry and wanted to increase their market share. During the initial years, efforts made to reduce cost through operational efficiency and sharing of platform cars enabled Nissan to come out of bankruptcy and for Renault to leverage Nissan's operational processes. But, with changing technology and increasing competition, it became critical for the partner firms to explore new technologies like hybrid cars and electric vehicles. Failure to reach to a consensus on alternative approaches would spell disaster for the alliance.

---

[2] Dawda, T. 2016. "On this Day in 2010 : When Mahindra bought out Renault's stake in their Joint Venture." April 16, 2016, http://autocarpro.in/feature/day-2010-mahindra-bought-renault-stake-joint-venture-11156 (accessed on July 31)

Partners might also have divergent objectives. For example, one partner might want to reinvest earnings of the venture for growth, whereas the other might want to receive dividends. One partner might want to diversify the product range, and the other might want to consolidate the business operations. A partner might also fear that an addition to the product range might compete with its wholly owned operations.

Nonsharing of Expertise and Knowledge by Managers

As mentioned in previous chapters, the stability of alliances is dependent on the continuous sharing of resources by the partner organizations and their consistent promised contribution to the alliance. Failure on behalf of one or both partners to share the promised resources and assets makes the partner organizations suspect the other's commitment to the alliance. This spoils the relationship between partners, which might consequently lead to termination of the alliance. In the case of Eli Lilly and Ranbaxy, the former's reluctance to set up a R&D lab in India and Ranbaxy further investing in other international joint ventures made both partners suspect each other's commitment to the alliance.

Inability of Parent Organizations to Share Control or Compromise on Difficult Issues

Who has a greater operational control in the alliance or commands the shots is always the bone of contention in most alliances. Partner firms might also differ with respect to differences in approach to a particular problem, thereby leading the partner organizations to reassess the benefits of continuing together. For example, the troubles plaguing AirAsia India, the alliance between Tata Sons and Air Asia India, led the former to deliberate on ending the partnership with Air Asia. Differences cropped up between the partners over operational control and the fact that the power of decision making lay wholly with the Malaysian parent. In addition, the alliance was troubled with respect to the mounting losses, allegations of financial irregularities, and illegal lobbying levied against the former CEO of the alliance.[3]

Breach of Trust by One of the Partner Organizations

Partners in an alliance are expected to honor the terms and conditions of the alliance. Failure to do so might lead to a breach of trust, which goes against the basic sentiment of a collaboration. For example, the joint venture agreement between the Wadia Group and Danone laid down that the popular *Tiger* brand would be used for products falling within the scope of the alliance in India. The Wadia group accused Danone for using the Tiger brand for products outside India. The Wadia group also objected to Danone investing in a bionutrition organization, without its knowledge. The government regulations laid down that a foreign organization needed the consent of its Indian partner before embarking on business ventures in similar areas. Breach of trust led to an uneasy relationship between the partner organization, thereby leading to the termination of the alliance.

Lack of Cultural Integration

The most challenging aspect of an alliance, especially a cross-cultural alliance, is to bring around an integration of diverse cultures. Failure to do so leads to partner organizations working as two isolated units. In such cases, partner organizations are also not able to draw synergies from the alliance. For example, the joint venture between GE and Godrej and Boyce, although lasted for seven years, partners parted ways on a bitter note, with the GE executives alleging that the Indian counterpart lacked professionalism. To top it, the products—high-capacity refrigerators and washing machines—that brought the two firms together failed to meet the expectations of the customers. The joint venture failed to achieve the projected

---

[3] Agarwal, S.C. 2018. "Tata Sons looks to end partnership with Air Asia, Enter Deal with Jet Airways." November 16, 2018 https://businesstoday.in/sectors/aviation/tata-sons-looks-to-end-partnership-with-airasia-enter-deal-with-jet-airways/story/291549.html (accessed August 31, 2019)

turnover, achieving just a quarter of the targeted sales. Lack of synergy between the partners led to termination. Similarly, the joint venture between American Express and a French luxury e-commerce company lasted for just three years. The French officials fell short of understanding the American market and the complete U.S. management team left the organization. The European cofounders did not like the efforts made to make the American website more user-friendly and did not understand the need for a Facebook Share button, something very normal for U.S. ecommerce sites.

Asymmetry in Contribution

In an alliance, dependency between partner organizations develops over time. Because one partner might learn more than the other, it might increase the dependency of the other partner on the former. The dependent partner may face a reversed bargaining situation. The disadvantaged partner may initiate renegotiation of contractual terms to maintain equal or more control on the alliance or leave the alliance altogether.

Uneven rate of resource exchange leads to vulnerability of joint ventures. Joint ventures are also said to have a "built-in self-destructing propensity." One approach to dealing with the mentioned problem is to structure the joint venture so as either to decrease the costs associated with continuing the alliance or to increase the costs associated with terminating the exchange.

Change in Competitive Strategy of One or Both Partners

A change in the competitive strategy has the potential to lead to a change in alliances. IBM had entered into alliances with Intel and Microsoft. When the demand for computer technology changed and Intel and Microsoft started exploiting their elevated positions at the expense of IBM, IBM suspended those ties and entered into alliance with Apple (Microsoft's future rival), Motorola (Intel's rival), and Siemens (a major rival of the Japanese firms pressurizing IBM for semiconductor technology). Similarly, the joint venture between Amtrex and Hitachi terminated because of change in business strategies. Whereas, Amtrex became more interested in consolidation of business, Hitachi was interested in product diversification.

It is, however, important for organizations to have a clear termination strategy so that the partner firms, even after termination, continue to maintain good relationship with each other.

Terms Governing Termination of Alliances

As discussed in the chapter of negotiations, it is very important for organizations to set out at the time of negotiations the contractual terms and conditions that will govern the termination of the alliance.

Identify Events that Will Trigger Termination

It is important that at the time of negotiations, the events that would trigger termination of the alliance are clearly identified and mentioned in the documents. Attainment of the objectives of the alliance or the alliance consistently failing to perform and attain objectives can trigger alliance termination. Change in the external environment, say government rules and regulations with respect to foreign direct investment (FDI) norms, can be another event that triggers termination. For example, a multinational organization forming a joint venture because of FDI norms always has a choice to exit the joint venture and set up a wholly owned subsidiary when 100 percent FDI is permitted. A change in the status of parents can again trigger a termination. For example, a parent getting acquired by a stronger player may have its strategic objectives laid as subordinate to the acquiring organization. The alliance may not fit into the overall corporate objective of the combined organization. The partner organization, in such circumstances, has a choice to terminate the alliance. In extreme cases, occurrence of a breach of trust or contract may trigger termination. It is important for the partner organization to reach a consensus with respect to events that would give a choice to both or either of the partners to call for termination of the alliance.

For example, in the alliance between Ginny and Johnny and the Future Group, any organization could exit from the alliance with three months of notice, after a minimum two years of lock-in period, in the following circumstances:

- Either is not satisfied with the performance
- Common output is not achieved

Chalk Out Clear HR Policies

Employees being a very critical stakeholder need to be assured of their job security and their career plans. Termination of alliances has a potential to jeopardize the career of executives. Executives involved in the alliance need to be assured of their future in case a joint venture is terminated. For example, in the case of joint venture between GE and SBI Caps, the executives having been contributed by SBI Caps were absorbed into SBI Caps after the joint venture terminated.

Determine Future Ownership Rights

An alliance, especially a joint venture, involves joint ownership of various resources and assets. Partners also transfer various resources to the alliance. At the time of termination, it becomes important to have a clarity on the continued ownership of the various assets. A partner contributing a technology to the alliance might like to take back the patent rights to the technology after termination. For example, in the case of Sony and Ericsson, post termination, Sony and Ericsson both took back the patent rights to the technology each had contributed to the joint venture. The ownership of the patents to the technology jointly developed by both partners was shared by both, post-termination. Even after termination, they continued to share the revenues generated from the jointly developed and owned technology. In case of termination of a co-marketing alliance, each firm would like to retain its own brands, customers, and other assets.

Reclaiming original assets in case of termination of joint ventures might be a challenge. The assets that are part of the joint venture would have been integrated into the functioning of the alliance and would cease to hold worth separately outside the joint venture. Therefore, the contract needs to mention specifically who will take ownership of the business and how the stakes of the existing partners would be valued. For example, the termination of the joint venture between Walmart and Bharti Enterprises in India led to both partners independently owning and operating different business formats. While Bharti Retail would own and operate *Easy Day* retail stores across all formats and grow the business, Walmart would continue to invest in the B2B Best Price Modern Wholesale Cash and Carry business.[4]

Determine the Method of Valuing Business

What method would be used for valuing the business at the time of termination is an important decision. Discounting cash flow method is one of the popular techniques that can be used for valuing the business. Organizations can also use the services of consultants or independent assessors such as an investment bank to set a price on the assets. Alternatively, predetermined price or pricing formula can be set for the business.

The price set, or the value of the business, determines the price that the buyer pays to the partners or the other partner for selling off its stake in the alliance.

Determine the Post-Termination Demands

It is also important for management executives to have a clarity on the terms and conditions that would govern the relationship between the partners, post termination. For example, when the joint venture between the Future Group and Ginny and Johnny terminated, it was agreed that they would continue in the relationship of a retailer and a vendor. Any restrictions to be placed on the partners post termination should be clearly defined. One of such restrictions can be a noncompete clause that blocks some or all the partners from competing in a particular product

---

[4] PTI. 2013. "Bharti Walmart Call off India JV; to Independently Pursue Retail Business." October 9, 2013, https://economictimes.indiatimes.com/industry / services/retail   /bharti-walmart-call-off-india-jv-to-independently-pursue-retail-business/articleshow/23782558.cms (accessed September 23, 2019)

or geography. In the joint venture formed between Sudhir Gensets and Cummins, a noncompete clause of three years post termination formed part of the joint venture negotiations. Similarly, in the Honda–Hero Motors joint venture, Honda had a three-year noncompeting clause in the bike segment, thereby forcing it to launch Activa, an electric scooter in the Indian market.

At times, alliances might have clauses laid down with respect to the future responsibilities that the partners would continue to have toward their customers, suppliers, or other parties.

A relevant question at this stage is: *Should the exit be easy (fast and inexpensive) or hard (lengthy and expensive)?* Hard exit terms and conditions may require an organization to pay a high premium to buyout its stake in the alliance, with the buyout spread over a number of months. On the other hand, an easy exit may require no capital transfers and only a month's termination notice. Hard exits could be effective in making parties more dedicated and committed to the relationship, thereby building trust. Easy exits, on the other hand, bring flexibility with regard to strategic decision making and resource allocation. A question following this argument is: *Should exit or hard provisions be uniform for all partners?* Probably, no. Exit provisions should, however, be clear and mutually decided by both the partners.

Possible Outcome of Alliance Termination Decisions

The organizations having reached to a consensus with respect to the termination of the alliance proceed with the legal formalities required for the termination. The termination decision may lead to the following.

Venture Being Liquidated Completely

In such a situation, the joint venture business may be dissolved, as partners see no value from the business and no third party is willing to buy the stake. There are practically no examples of joint venture organizations being liquidated and assets being sold off. In most of the alliances, one or the other partners buy over the assets of the alliance. In the joint venture between Unitech and the Telenor group, named Uninor, because of the government canceling licenses of a number of telecom operators, the joint venture organization was forced to shut down its operations in a number of states. Unitech exited the joint venture with the Telenor group buying over the entire stake. Airtel later on bought over Telenor India. Another example could be the alliance between Bajaj and Renault–Nissan to produce a car costing less than the Nano car so as to be directly in competition with Tata Motors. Due to lack of clarity in the alliance objectives and the delegation of roles and responsibilities between the partners, the alliance was terminated and the venture abandoned.

Venture Sold to the Local Partner

The second possibility is where after the termination of the alliance, the multinational player exits from the alliance and its stake is bought over by the local partner. For example, the alliance between TVS Motors and Suzuki when it was called off because of differing objectives of the two partners TVS Motors bought over Suzuki's stake in the joint venture. Here it is assumed that the local player feels confident of continuing with the venture without the presence of the multinational player. Likewise, in the joint venture Kinetic Honda Ltd., Kinetic Engineering Ltd. bought out Honda's stake in the venture.

Multinational Enterprise Buys Out Its Joint Venture Partner and Forms a Wholly Owned Subsidiary

The third possibility is that the multinational enterprise may decide to buy the stake of the local partner in the alliance and form a wholly owned subsidiary in the foreign country. The multinational organization might find that the advantages of a globally integrated value chain outweigh the benefits of having a local partner. The multinational organization, because of its operations in the international market, would not only have learned the tricks of the trade in that country from the local partner, but would also be convinced of the potential of the market. For example, when IBM re-entered into India, in the postliberalization era, it entered by forming a joint venture with Tata Information Systems Ltd. When it became more confident of its operations in the Indian market, it bought over Tata's stake and set up its wholly owned subsidary, IBM India Private Limited. A similar example can be taken of the Escorts Yamaha Ltd. joint venture. It started out as a 50:50 joint venture between Escorts India Ltd. and Yamaha Motor Corporation. In 2000, the investment ratio was changed to 74 percent for Yamaha and 26 percent for Escorts. In 2001, Yamaha Motor Corporation acquired the remaining 26 percent of the stocks held by Escorts to make Yamaha Escorts Ltd. a 100 percent subsidiary of Yamaha Motor Corporation.

Can either of the partners make exit difficult for the other? Yes, a partner dependent on the resources of the other partner might like to tie up the latter to the alliance and make the partner's exit from the alliance difficult. Honda was forced to sell its stake to Hero Motors at a discount of 30 to 50 percent.

Venture Sold to Outsiders

In contrast to the first possibility, the venture organization might be sold to outside parties. In this case, either of the partners see less possibility of creating value from the alliance. On the other hand, the third party would be anticipating to create value for its business by leveraging the assets. In case the partner organizations are desperate to get out of the alliance, the third party might be the gainer by getting the assets at below market price. For example, when the alliance between SPIC and Henkel terminated, neither of the partner found it worthwhile to buy the assets of the venture. They were able to find a third party, Jyothi Laboratories, that bought over the stake in the venture.

In all the mentioned strategic moves, what is it that management executives need to keep in mind? An organization's decision to continue or not to continue with the alliance is based on its predicted cash flows and value from the alliance. For example, an organization may decide to buy out the partner organization's stake in the joint venture if the price it has to pay for exercising its right to acquire the stake is less than the predicted value of the cash flows it can generate from the alliance. Similarly, an organization may decide to sell its stake in the alliance if the money it is getting by selling the alliance is more than the predicted value of the cash flows it would be able to generate in case it continues to hold onto the alliance. The organization can always invest the funds generated from the sale into an alternative business venture that helps it to generate more returns.

How is the exercise price determined? It can be stated as (i) *a priori* fixed price, (ii) according to the rules of calculation agreed in the contract, or on the (iii) market price.

Having discussed termination of alliances, an important question for management executives to ponder is: *Does the stock market reflect joint venture termination announcements?* Probably, yes. The stock market takes a negative view of alliances that are terminated due to cultural differences. Alliances terminated wherein continuation would result in a lower net predicted value than when terminated would result in the increase in the stock price. For example, the termination of the joint venture between Sony and Ericsson led to an increase in the stock price of Ericsson as the investors in Ericsson's share anticipated that the money put back into Ericsson's core business would lead to higher returns than what would have resulted if Ericsson would have continued with the alliance.

An important question is: *Is every alliance termination a failure?* Probably not. It depends on the performance expectations set and the extent they have been met. As alliances are used as vehicles for exploring new opportunities, it is not surprising that some prove to be less rewarding than initially expected. An important point of deliberation here could be: How do we rate an alliance that continues to exist even after it has ceased producing value? Or, how do we rate an alliance where no expectations are set and hence no value created?

Can strategic planning lead to failure of an alliance? Probably, yes, if the planning is driven by a rush to form an alliance without clearly identifying the value to be created from the alliance or setting the performance criteria. Lack of due diligence exercise to identify the right partner for the alliance might either lead to waste of alliance resources or improper exploitation of the surplus alliance resources. Management executives failing in clearly articulating alliance exit conditions and processes might also contribute to the failure of an alliance.

As illustrated in Figure 8.1 assessing the joint venture and taking adequate decisions is critical. Every alliance tends to follow a lifecycle. An alliance will decline if it does not remain relevant in the market. Termination should be a well-thought-out decision. In fact, organizations that strategically think about termination create more value from an alliance *vis-à-vis* organizations that spend all their energy in deliberating on the terms and condition governing the formation of the alliance. It is always advisable for partner organizations to part ways on amicable terms, leaving possibility of partnering in future.

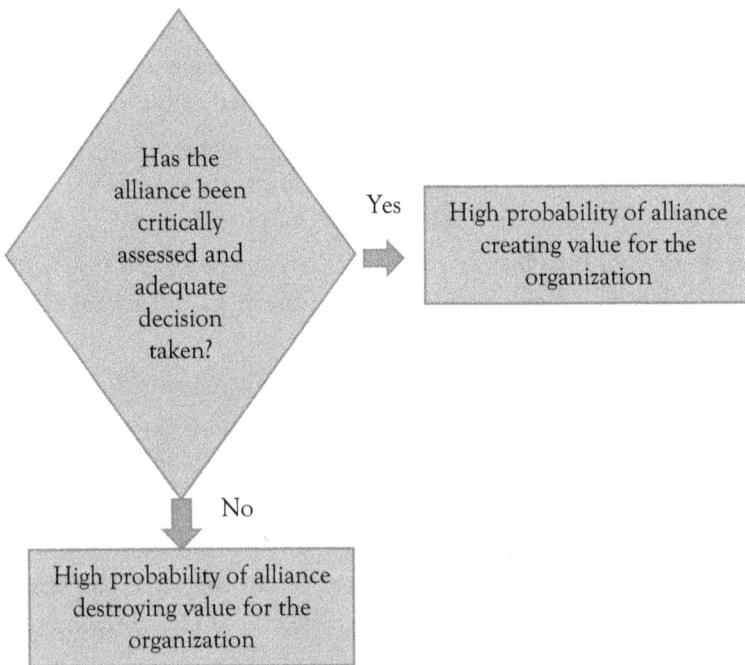

Figure 8.1 Alliance assessment outcomes

CHAPTER 9

Alliance or Acquisition

Not having the resources or capabilities to go ahead independently drives managerial executives to either go for an alliance or acquisition. Interestingly, although executives talk about acquisitions and alliances in the same breath, few address them as alternative channels by which organizations can attain objectives. Most organizations do not compare the two strategies, resulting in they entering into collaborations when they should have acquired or vice-versa.

Having understood the lifecycle of an alliance, a point worth debating at this stage is why do organizations decide to go for an alliance and not for an acquisition or vice-versa. For example as illustrated in Figure 9.1, why did Microsoft enter into an alliance, in February 2011, with Nokia before it went ahead and acquired its core cellphone business in September 2013. If Microsoft needed Nokia's mobile handset technology, why had it not simply bought it in 2011?

Although organizations have still not been able to master the dilemma between when to acquire other organizations or ally with them, a few indicative factors can help managerial executives to streamline their thinking. Executives need to analyze certain factors before deciding on a collaboration or acquisition option.

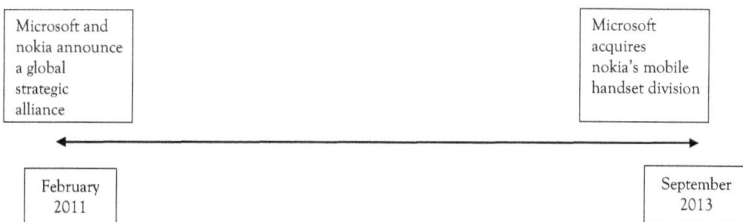

Figure 9.1 Staged strategic approach of Microsoft

Indicative Factors—Ally or Acquire?

Indivisibility of Assets or Resources

Whether or not the assets or resources possessed by the target organization, (A) divisible or not is an important question before management executives of the organization on the lookout for resources (B). In case assets are indivisible and cannot be separated from A, B has no choice but to get access to the whole of A. For example, if B needs the distribution network of A, B knows that the distribution network is not a standalone asset removed from A. In this case, if B decided to go and acquire A, the former will be unnecessarily burdened with a lot of assets and liabilities that B does not require. In such a situation, it is advisable for B to get into an alliance with A to share the distribution network as part of the alliance agreement. On the contrary, if it is possible to carve out the asset in need from A and do a valuation of the standalone asset, B might consider acquiring the asset from A. This is an important decision, especially where the target organization is large sized and acquiring it might place a lot of unnecessary burden on the acquiring organization.

Management Costs of an Acquisition

It is a known fact that acquisitions are costly decisions with costs involved in the conduct of due diligence exercise preacquisition, costs involved in financing, and integration postacquisition. Many organizations become highly leveraged in financing an acquisition deal. In case B has deep pockets and has minimal financial risk involved, B can still go ahead and acquire A. But, in case B lacks sufficient financial resources, an alliance with A would be better for B.

Difficulties in Assessing Value of Target Organization

An acquisition deal demands doing a rigorous due diligence exercise to do an accurate valuation of the target organization. Any kind of information asymmetry defeats the purpose. The challenge in assessing the value of the target organization is especially pronounced in cases where the target organization is unlisted. In such a situation, the risk of overpaying for the target organization, more than the anticipated synergies from the deal, runs high. An organization can avoid the risk by going for an alliance with the target organization. In case B is confident of the valuation of A, and the potential synergies, it can still go ahead with acquiring A.

Governmental and Institutional Barrier

Industries and organizations in many countries are protected by government rules and regulations. For example, FDI norms limit the maximum stake a multinational can own in a local organization. Or, in many instances, a multination organization might face an entry barrier with respect to the connect customers might have with the local players. In such cases, entry into an international market is advisable by getting into an alliance, rather than going for an acquisition.

Cultural Differences

Majority of strategic alliances and acquisitions fail because of lack of cultural integration. The costs involved in the failure of an acquisition are much more than the costs involved in the failure of an alliance. Where the cultural differences between two organizations are stark, it is advisable to go for an alliance, rather than going for an acquisition.

Resources or Synergies Desired

Organizations when debating on the alliance or acquisition decision should deliberate on the key resources required from the deal and the synergies desired. Key resources required might be hard resources like plant and machinery, real assets, or distribution network, or soft resources like skills and expertise of employees. When organizations desire to gain access to soft resources, especially human resources, it is advisable to go for an alliance rather than acquisition. An acquisition demotivates employees, leading to key employees leaving the organization.

Similarly, synergies desired might be modular, sequential, or reciprocal synergies. Modular synergies are achieved when resources are managed independently, only the results are pooled for greater profits. For example, when a retail outlet and a credit card company collaborate with each other, it allows a customer to encash the points accumulated from use of the credit card at the retail outlet, thereby benefitting both the credit card company and the retail outlet. In such cases, a simple nonequity contractual alliance will serve the purpose for both organizations. Sequential synergies are realized when one organization does its tasks and passes on the output to the other organization to do its bit. In this case, the resources of the two organizations are sequentially interdependent. For example, when an automobile component manufacturer enters into an alliance with an automobile manufacturer, both are looking out for sequential synergies. A rigidly drafted contractual agreement or an equity alliance will help the organizations derive the synergies. Organizations generate reciprocal synergies only by working together and performing tasks through an interactive knowledge-sharing session. In such cases, organizations might be required not only to combine the resources, but also customize them to make them reciprocally interdependent. For organizations targeting reciprocal synergies, an acquisition might work out to be better than an alliance.

Another lens through which resources can be looked at it is whether the organizations will be burdened with redundant resources by teaming up with the other organization. These surplus resources can be used to generate economies of scale or can be used to cut costs by eliminating those resources. In case of redundant resources, it is advisable for organizations to go for an acquisition.

Competition and Uncertainty in the Marketplace

Many organizations are of the impression that an acquisition or an alliance decision is an internal matter, thereby failing to take into account external factors like competition or uncertainty in the marketplace due to customer behavior or success of a particular technology. In case of an uncertain market, it becomes challenging to gauge accurately the payoffs from a particular strategic decision. Therefore, in cases where uncertainty is very high, going ahead with an acquisition decision might be a risky affair. In such cases, the organization should go for a strategic alliance, rather than an acquisition. On the other hand, if the competition in the market is intense, an organization, in order to preempt similar moves from other players, might like to go and acquire the target organization.

Competencies at Collaborating or Acquiring

Historically, if an organization has entered into strategic alliances in the past and has developed skills and competencies at collaborating, it might feel more confident of going ahead with a strategic alliance. Similarly, if an organization has believed in acquiring organizations to achieve objectives rather than going for alliances, it will be able to create more value out of an acquisition. Managing a strategic alliance for the organization might become a challenging task. Organizations create knowledge repositories based on their learnings from various strategic decisions and leverage these learnings in subsequent decisions. For example, a renowned multinational organization that had always followed an approach of acquiring organizations failed miserably when it entered into a strategic alliance.

As compared to an acquisition a strategic alliance demands sharing of control over various matters and strategic decisions. An organization that aspires to have full control over the operations and wants to be in total command of various strategic decisions should go for acquiring the target organization, rather than going for an alliance.

An important point that executives need to keep in mind is that the aforementioned factors do not work in isolation. A holistic perspective is required after taking into account all the factors, to reach to a decision whether an organization should go ahead with an alliance or acquisition.

To conclude, let us return to our deal between Microsoft and Nokia. Why did Microsoft follow a staged approach to acquiring Nokia? Why did it not acquire Nokia in the first instance? As is evident from the following framework illustrated in Figure 9.2, most of the factors are pointing toward an acquisition being the right strategic move for Microsoft in 2011. Microsoft, maybe, wanted to explore the market better before going ahead with an acquisition decision. The alliance survived for around two years, subsequent to which it led to an acquisition of Nokia by Microsoft.

Management executives also need to keep in mind that at the point of taking decision, the target organization should also agree to sell off its business unit or assets under discussion. If the target organizations, in our case Nokia, feels in the first instance that it should continue holding onto its mobile handset division as it can extract value from it, it would not agree to an acquisition offer from the acquiring company, Microsoft. And, in case Microsoft also sees no credit in going for a hostile takeover, it would prefer to get into an alliance to get access to the resources.

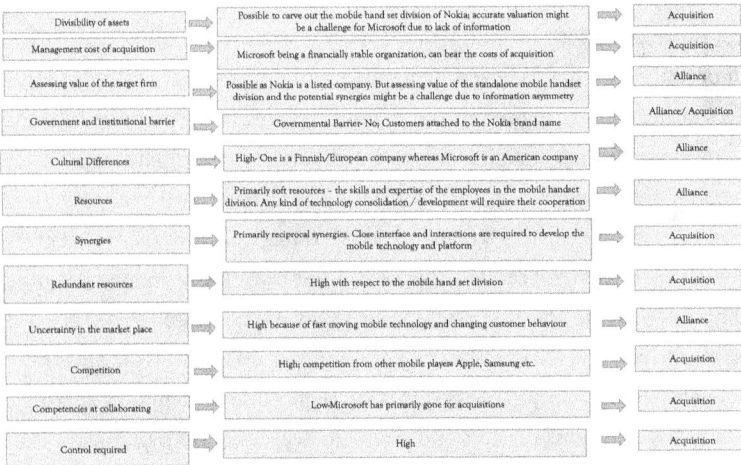

Factor	Description	Recommendation
Divisibility of assets	Possible to carve out the mobile hand set division of Nokia; accurate valuation might be a challenge for Microsoft due to lack of information	Acquisition
Management cost of acquisition	Microsoft being a financially stable organization, can bear the costs of acquisition	Acquisition
Assessing value of the target firm	Possible as Nokia is a listed company. But assessing value of the standalone mobile handset division and the potential synergies might be a challenge due to information asymmetry	Alliance
Government and institutional barrier	Governmental Barrier- No; Customers attached to the Nokia brand name	Alliance/ Acquisition
Cultural Differences	High- One is a Finnish/European company whereas Microsoft is an American company	Alliance
Resources	Primarily soft resources - the skills and expertise of the employees in the mobile handset division. Any kind of technology consolidation / development will require their cooperation	Alliance
Synergies	Primarily reciprocal synergies. Close interface and interactions are required to develop the mobile technology and platform	Acquisition
Redundant resources	High with respect to the mobile hand set division	Acquisition
Uncertainty in the market place	High because of fast moving mobile technology and changing customer behaviour	Alliance
Competition	High; competition from other mobile players Apple, Samsung etc.	Acquisition
Competencies at collaborating	Low-Microsoft has primarily gone for acquisitions	Acquisition
Control required	High	Acquisition

Figure 9.2 Acquire or Ally: Microsoft and Nokia

CHAPTER 10

Conclusion

Having gone through the complete lifecycle of an alliance, it is evident that alliances are becoming the core of corporate strategy decisions of organizations and need to be given a deep thought. That in the current dynamic environment strategic alliances are becoming inevitable, focus of management executives should be how to make their alliances succeed. Efforts need to be made to ensure that the alliance performance meets corporate expectations. Being able to form and manage alliances better than competitors can serve an important source of competitive advantage. Even though the objective of the alliance may be to develop new markets, new technology, or new knowledge, there is no surety of doing so. A strong alliance orientation, that is the ability to scan the environment for alliance opportunities, to coordinate the activities across different alliances, and to learn from the experiences of various alliances, is required for higher alliance performance.

It can be summarized that for an alliance to be successful, it is important that the partners have:

Clarity of Strategic Purpose

Clarity of the strategic purpose or the business case for the alliance is very important for a stable alliance. Companies getting into an alliance without having a clarity how it feeds into the overall corporate strategy of their organization will not be able to create value from the alliance. The possibility of alliance being instable runs high, thereby destroying any value that could have been created.

Compatibility and Complementarity

Strategic alliances survive on complementarity between the partners. Organizations should complement each other with respect to resources contributed or competencies linked together. Also, it is important that the partners are compatible with each other not only with respect to interpersonal relationships, but also with respect to their goals and strategic agenda.

Clear Identification of the Value to Be Created

Organizations in an alliance will continue to be together till they see independent and joint value getting created from the alliance. It is, therefore, very important to have a clarity with respect to the value the partners anticipate to create from the alliance. Not having a clarity will lead to partners taking decisions that do not feed into either the strategy of the alliance or that of the parent organizations.

Clear Identification of Risks Involved

As discussed in the chapters, even though an alliance gets formed to share the risks of business involved, each alliance faces a number of risks—be it with respect to inter-partner relationships or with respect to sharing of resources. Companies getting into an alliance should identify clearly the risks involved so that measures can be taken to ward off the risks. Not identifying the potential risks during the course of the alliance might find the partners unprepared to manage them. This might lead to instability in the alliance and further termination if not handled strategically.

Clear Allocation of Tasks and Responsibilities

We would not like a partner free-riding on the contributions of other partners. Therefore, it is very important that the tasks and responsibilities of each partner gets clearly defined and allocated. Failure to do so might lead to confusion in the operations of the alliance. It might lead to delayed decision making and the alliance losing competitive edge *vis-à-vis* rivals in the industry.

Incentives for Cooperation

Alliance management is not a simple and straightforward job. In order to ensure that the alliance manager acts as a true agent of the parent organizations, it is important that he or she is given the right kind of incentives. For the success of a joint venture, it is important that the joint venture alliance manager sees his or her allegiance to the joint venture first and to the parents second. Employees involved in the alliance also need to be assured of a security to their job and profile within the organization in case of alliance termination.

Clear Identification of Performance Expectations

Linked to the expectation of value from the alliance is a performance metric that gives a mechanism to control the alliance outcome. Partners in an alliance should clearly lay down the performance expectations from the alliance—be it in terms of strategic, financial, or learning outcomes. Care needs to be taken that the expectations set down are not unrealistic. Inability to lay down clear performance parameters might lead to absence of a control mechanism and an inability to assess the value being created from the alliance.

Creating a Dedicated Alliance Function

A dedicated alliance function coordinates all the alliance-related activities in an organization and is given the task of institutionalizing processes and systems to share and leverage prior experience of alliance management and know-how throughout the organization. An alliance function also facilitates the sharing of tacit knowledge through training programs and internal networks of alliance managers. Dyer, Kale, and Singh in their research discovered that organizations with a dedicated alliance function achieved a 25 percent higher long-term success rate with their alliances and generated four times the market wealth whenever they announced the formation of an alliance as compared to organizations without such a function. Such organizations are also able to attract better partners and form more alliances.

Building Trust Should Be the First Priority

Establishing a trust-based relationship is critical for ensuring success of the alliance. Trust drives the commitment of valuable resources and know-how to the partnership. Trust building is a time-consuming process and is developed through positive experiences in the early stages and through jointly solving problems over time. Management executives should leverage every opportunity to create a positive climate and establish a reliable flow of communication.

Bibliography

Adarkar, A., A. Adil, D. Ernst, and P. Vaish. 1997. "Emerging Market Alliances: Must they Be Win-Lose?" *McKinsey Quarterly*, no. 4, pp. 120–137.

Adobor, H., and R.S. McMullen. March-April 2002. "Strategic Partnering in E-commerce: Guidelines for Managing Alliances." *Business Horizon* 45, no. 2, pp. 67–76.

Akhavan, P., S. Barak, H. Maghsoudlou, and J. Antucheviciene. March 2015. "FQSPM-SWOT for Strategic Alliance Planning and Partner Selection: Case Study in a Holding Car Manufacturer Company." *Technological and Economic Development of Economy* 21, no. 2, pp. 165–185.

Anslinger, P., and J. Jenk. April 2004. "Creating Successful Alliances." *Journal of Business Strategy* 25, no. 2, pp. 18–22.

Austin, J.E. 2000. *The Collaboration Challenge: How Nonprofits and Businesses Succeed through Strategic Alliances.* San Francisco,CA :Jossey-Bass.

Badaracco, J.L., Jr. 1998. *General Motor's Asian Alliances.* Harvard Business School Case.

Bamford, J., D. Ernst, and D.G. Fubini. February 2004. "Launching a World Class Joint Venture." *Harvard Business Review* 82, no. 2, pp. 90–100.

Bamford, J.D., B. Gomes-Casseres, and M.S. Robinson. 2003. *Mastering Alliance Strategy: A Comprehensive Guide to Design, Management, and Organization,* 63–115. San Francisco: CA,:John Wiley & Sons Inc.

Barger, B.B. 2007. "Culture an Overused Term and International Joint Ventures: A Review of the Literature." *Journal of Organizational Culture, Communication and Conflict* 11, no. 2, pp. 1–14

Beamish, P.W., and N. Lupton. May 2009. "Managing Joint Ventures." *Academy of Management Perspectives* 23, no. 2, pp. 75–94.

Bener, M., and K.W. Glaister. 2010. "Determinants of Performance in International Joint Ventures." *Journal of Strategy and Management* 3, no. 3, pp. 188–214.

Bouncken, R.B., and V. Fredrich. November 2016. "Good Fences Make Good Neighbours? Directions and Safeguards in Alliances on Business Model Innovation." *Journal of Business Research* 69, no. 11, pp. 5196–5202.

Brian T., P. Vos, and K. Burgers. 2012. *Strategic Alliance Management by Brian Tjemkes, pepijn Vos and Koen Burgers.* Routledge.

Burgelman, R., and S. Leslie. 2008. "The Renault-Nissan Alliance in 2008: Exploiting the Potential of a Novel Organizational Form." *Stanford Graduate School of Business,* SM166.

Calontone, R., and Y. Sam Zhao. March 2001. "Joint ventures in China: A comparative study of Japanese, Korean and U.S. Partners." *Journal of International Marketing* 9, no. 1, pp. 1–23.

Chang, S.C., S.S. Chen, and J.H. Lai. April 2008. "The Effect of Alliance Experience and Intellectual Capital on the Value Creation of International Strategic Alliances." *Omega* 36, no. 2, pp. 298–316.

Cui, A.S., and G. O'Connor. July 2012. "Alliance Portfolio Resource Diversity and Firm Innovation." *Journal of Marketing* 76, pp. 24–43.

Cummings, J.L., and S.R. Holmberg. April-June 2012. "Best-Fit Alliance Partners: The Use of Critical Success Factors in a Comprehensive Partner Selection Process." *Long Range Planning* 45, no. 2–3, pp. 136–159.

Das, T.K., and B.S. Teng. July 1998. "Between Trust and Control: Building Confidence in Partner Cooperation in Alliances." *The Academy of Management Review* 23, no. 3, pp. 491–512.

Das, T.K., and B.S. Teng. November 1999. "Managing Risks in Strategic Alliances." Academy of Management Executive 13, no. 4, pp. 50–62.

Das, T.K., and B.S. Teng. November 1996. "Risk Types and Inter-Firm Alliance Structures." *Journal of Management Studies* 33, pp. 827–843.

Das, T.K., and R. Kumar. September 2011. "Inter-Partner Negotiations in Alliances: A Strategic Framework." *Management Decision* 49, no. 8, pp. 1235–1256.

Das, T.K. June 2005. "Deceitful Behaviors of Alliance Partners: Potential and Prevention." *Management Decision* 43, no. 5, pp. 706–719.

Dasgupta, M. September 2018. "Driving Innovation Through Strategic Alliances: A Framework." *International Journal of Strategic Business Alliances* 6, no. 3, pp. 130–147.

Dhanaraj, C. and P.W. Beamish. 2004. "Effect of Equity Ownership on the Survival of International Joint Ventures." *Strategic Management Journal* 25, no. 3, pp. 295–305.

Doz Yves, L., and G. Hamel. 1998. *Alliance Advantage: The Art of Creating Value Through Partnering*. Boston: Harvard Business Press.

Duisters, D., G. Duysters, D. Pieter, and A. Man. n.d. "A Study into the Role of a Partner Selection Process in Alliance Capability Building." As accessed from https://researchgate.net/publication /228432234_A_study_into_the_role_of_a_partner_selection_process_in_alliance_capability_building

Dyer, J.H., P. Kale, and H. Singh. July–August 2004. "When to Ally, When to Acquire." *Top-Line Growth*, pp. 108–115.

Dyer, J.H., P. Kale, and H. Singh. July 2001. "How to Make Strategic Alliances Work." *MIT Sloan Management Review* 42, no. 4, pp. 37–43.

Emden, Z., R.J Calantone and C. Droge. July 2006. "Collaborating for New Product Development: Selecting the Partner with Maximum Potential to Create Value." *The Journal of Product Innovation Management* 23, no. 4, pp. 330–341.

Esen, A., and G. Alpay. June 2017. "Exploring the Impact of Firm and Relationship Specific Factors on Alliance Performance: Evidence from Turkey." *South African Journal of Business Management* 48, no. 2, pp. 11–21.

Gulati, R., and H. Singh. December 1998. "The Architecture of Cooperation: Managing Coordination Costs and Appropriation Concerns in Strategic Alliances." *Administrative Science Quarterly* 43, no. 4, pp. 781–814.

Gulati, R., M. Sytch, and P. Mehrotra. July 2008. "Breaking Up is Never Easy: Planning for Exit in a Strategic Alliance." *California Management Review* 50, no. 4, pp. 147–163.

Gulati, R., M. Sytch, and R. Tahilyani. 2014. "Indus Towers: From Infancy to Maturity." *Harvard Business School.*

Gulati, R. December 1998. "Alliances and Networks." *Strategic Management Journal* 19, no. 4, pp. 293–317.

Hamel, G. Summer 1991. "Competition for Competence and Inter-Partner Learning Within International Strategic Alliances." *Strategic Management Journal* 12, no. 51, pp. 83–103.

Harrigan, K.R. 1985a. *Strategies for Joint Ventures.* Lexington MA, Lexington Books.

Harvey, M.G., and R.F. Lusch. June 1995. "A Systematic Assessment of Potential International Strategic Alliance Partners." *International Business Review* 4, no. 2, pp. 195–212.

Hitt, M.A., T. Dacin, E. Levitas, J.L. Arregle, and A. Borza. June 2000. "Partner Selection in Emerging and Developed Market Contexts: Resource Based and Organizational Learning Perspectives." *Academy of Management Journal* 43, no. 3, pp. 449–467.

Hoang, H., and F.T. Rothaermal. August 2016. "How to Manage Alliances Strategically." *MIT Sloan Management Review*, pp. 68–76.

Hofstde, G. 2010. "Cultures and Organizations." *Software of the Mind.* Berkshire, U.K.:McGraw Hill.

Industries, pp. 315–344. Harvard Business School Press,

Inkpen, A.C., and P.W. Beamish. January 1997. "Knowledge, Bargaining Power, and the Instability of International Joint Ventures." *The Academy of Management Review* 22, no. 1, pp. 177–202.

Kang, J. September 2014. "Understanding the Roles of Trust at Different Stages in Strategic Alliances: A Theoretical Review." *Business Management Dynamics* 4, no. 3, pp. 1–14.

Kayo, E., H. Kimura, M.R. Patrocinio, and L. Elesbao de Oliveira Neto. (2010). "Acquisitions, joint ventures or arm's length alliances? Analyzing the determinants of the choice of growth strategy in Brazil from 1996 through 2007", *Brazilian Administration Review* 7, no. 4, pp. 397–412.

Kester, W.C. March/April 1984. "Today's Options for Tomorrow's Growth." *Harvard Business Review* 62, pp. 153–160.

Killing, J.P. 1988. "Understanding Alliances: The Role of Task and Organizational Complexity." In *Cooperative Strategies in International Business*, eds. F. Contractor, and P. Lorange, 55–67, Lexington, MA: Lexington Books.

Kim, C., W. Zhan, and M.K. Erramilli. July 2011. "Resources and Performance of International Joint Ventures: The Moderating Role of Absorptive Capacity." *Journal of Asia Business Studies* 5, no. 2, pp. 145–160.

Kittilaksanawong, W., and C. Palecki. 2015. "Renault-Nissan Alliance : Will Further Integration Create More Synergies?" *Ivey Publishing*.

Klein, S., and C. Dev. July 1997. "Partner Selection in Market-Driven Strategic Alliances." *South African Journal of Business Management* 28, no. 3, pp. 97–104.

Kogut, B. January 1991. "Joint Ventures and the Option to Expand and Acquire." *Management Science* 37, no. 1, pp. 19–33.

Kumar, R. August 2014. "Managing Ambiguity in Strategic Alliances." *CMRBerkeley Edu*, 56, no. 4, pp. 62–102.

Ladika, S. 2018. *The Worldwide Workforce: Can Companies Train the Talent Needed for a Global Economy in Issues in Management*. Sage Publications: Los Angeles, 2018.

Lawrence, S. 2005. *Handle with Care: Negotiating Strategic Alliances*. Harvard Business School Publishing.

Lee, J.R., W.R. Chen, and C. Kao. October 2003. "Determinants and Performance Impact of Asymmetric Governance Structures in International Joint Ventures: An Empirical Investigation." *Journal of Business Research* 56, no. 10, pp. 815–828.

Li, J., K.R. Xin, A. Tsui, and D.C. Hambrick. 1999. "Building Effective International Joint Venture Leadership Teams in China." *Journal of World Business* 34, no. 1, pp. 52–68.

Hill, L.A. August 1999. "What it Really Means to Manage: Exercising Power and Influence." *HBS No. 9-400-041*

Luehrman, T.A. September-October 1998. "Strategy as a Portfolio of Real Options." *Harvard Business Review*, pp. 89–99.

Merchant, H., and D. Schendel. June 2000. "How Do International Joint Ventures Create Shareholder Value?" *Strategic Management Journal* 21, no. 7, pp. 723–737.

Merchant, H. November 2014. "Configurations of Governance Structure, Generic Strategy, and Firm Size: Opening the Black Box of Value Creation in International Joint Ventures." *Global Strategy Journal* 4, no. 4, pp. 292–309.

Mitsuhashi, H., and H.R. Greve. November 2009. "A Matching Theory of Alliance Formation and Organizational Success: Complementarity and Compatibility." *Academy of Management Journal* 52, no. 5, pp. 975–999.

Moreira, S. 2018. "How to Hook Knowledge When Angling for Innovation: Learning Through Licensing." *IESE Business School*, no. 36, pp. 29–35.

Overby, M.L. August 2009. "Partner Selection Criteria in Strategic Alliances: When to Ally with Weak Partners." https://pdfs.semanticscholar.org/7a31/aeff5b954d09f00bea30cc16920c8a8c5b8a.pdf

Oxley, J.E., and R.C. Sampson. July 2004. "The Scope and Governance of International R&D Alliances." *Strategic Management Journal* 25, no. 8–9, pp. 723–749.

Ozorhon, B., D. Arditi, I. Dikmen, and M.T. Birgonul. May 2008. "Implications of Culture in the Performance of International Construction Joint Ventures." *Journal of Construction Engineering and Management* 134, no. 5, p. 361

Pankaj, D. October 15, 2013. "SingTel looks to Buy Out Allies in Joint Venture." https://timesofindia.indiatimes.com/business/india-business/SingTel-looks-to-buy-out-allies-in-joint-venture/articleshow/24173124.cms

Park, S.H., and M.V. Russo. June 1996. "When Competition Eclipses Cooperation: An Event History Analysis of Joint Venture Failure." *Management Science* 42, no. 6, pp. 875–890.

Petrovic, J., A. Kakabadse, N.K Kakabadse. March 2006. "International Joint Venture (IJV) Directors' Contribution to Board Effectiveness: Learning from the Literature." *Management Decision* 44, no. 3, pp. 346–366.

Porter, M. E. and M. B. Fuller (1986). 'Coalitions and global

Porter, M.E., and M.J. Fuller. 1986. "Coalitions and Global Strategy." In *Competition in Global Industries*, ed. M.E. Porter, 315–344. Boston MA: Harvard Business School Press.

Porter, P.D., V.F. Sheckler, and G.H. Im. May 2003. "Negotiating Bio-Technology Strategic Alliances." *The Licensing Journal*, pp. 1–8.

Prahalad,C.K., and M.S. Krishnan. 2008. *The New Age of Innovation:Driving Cocreated Value Through Global Networks*. McGraw Hill, United States of America.

Ramaswamy, K. January 2009. "Renault-Nissan: The Challenge of Sustaining Strategic Change." *Thunderbird School of Management,* TB0047.

Reur, J., and S.V. Devarakonda. March 2008. "Does My Partnership Need a Joint Steering Committee? Governance in Non-Equity Alliances." *IESE Business School* 36.

Robson, M.J., C.S. Katsikeas, and D.C. Bello. July-August 2008. "Drivers and Performance Outcomes of Trust in International Strategic Alliances: The Role of Organizational Complexity." *Organization Science* 19, no. 4, pp. 647–665.

Sarkar, M.**B.**, R. Echambadi, S.T. Cavusgil, and P.S. Aulakh. September 2001. "The Influence of Complementary, Compatibility, and Relational Capital on Alliance Performance." *Journal of the Academy of Marketing Sciences* 29, no. 4, pp. 358–373.

Schaan, J.L., and M.J. Kelly. *Cases in Alliance Management: Building Successful Alliances.* United States of America:Sage Publications inc.

Segil, L. 2004. "Can this Partnership be Saved? Getting an Alliance Back on Track." In *Negotiating and Managing Partnerships*, 41–42. The Harvard Business School Publishing.

Segil, L. 2004. "Trying It on for Size." In *Negotiating and Managing Partnerships.* The Harvard Business School Publishing, pp. 37–38.

Shah, R.H., and V. Swaminathan. March 2008. "Factors Influencing Partner Selection in Strategic Alliances: The Moderating Role of Alliance Context." *Strategic Management Journal* 29, no. 5, pp. 471–494.

Shih, W., G. Pissano, and A. King. 2008. *Radical Collaboration: IBM Microelectronics Joint Development Alliances*. Ivey Publishing.

Si, S.X., and G.D. Bruton. February 1999. "Knowledge Transfer in International Joint Ventures in Transitional Economies: The China Experience." *The Academy of Management Executive* 13, no. 1, pp. 83–90.

Solesvik, M.Z., and P. Westhead. June 2010. "Partner Selection for Strategic Alliances: Case Study Insights from the Maritime Industry." *Industrial Management and Data Systems* 110, no. 6, pp. 841–860.

strategy'. In: M. E. Porter (ed.), Competition in Global

Suen, W.W. 2005. *Non-Cooperation: The Dark Side of Strategic Alliances*. Palgrave Macmillan, UK.

Swoboda, B., M. Meierer, T. Foscht, and D. Morschett. August 2011. "International SME Alliances: The Impact of Alliance Building and Configurational Fit on Success." *Long Range Planning* 44, no. 4, pp. 271–288.

Swoboda, B., S. Elsner, and E. Olejnik. June 2015. "How do Past Mode Choices Influence Subsequent Entry? A Study on the Boundary Conditions of Preferred Entry Modes of Retail Firms." *International Business Review* 24, no. 3, pp. 506–517.

Taylor, A. May 2005. "An Operations Perspective on Strategic Alliance Success Factors." *International Journal of Operations & Product Management* 25, nos. 5/6, pp. 469–490.

Teece, D.J. June 1992. "Competition, Cooperation and Innovation: Organizational Arrangements for Regimes of Rapid Technological Progress." *Journal of Economic Behavior and Organization* 18, no. 1, pp. 1–25.

Tiziana, C., and C. Darwall. April 2003. *The HP-Cisco Alliance (A)*. Ivey Publishing .

Tong, T.W., J.J. Reuer, and M.W. Peng. October 2008. "International Joint Ventures and the Value of Growth Options." *Academy of management Journal* 51, no. 5, pp. 1014–1029.

Tong, T.W., and J.J. Reur. August 2010. "Competitive Consequences of Inter-firm Collaboration: How Joint Ventures Shape Industry Profitability." *Journal of International Business Studies* 41, no. 6, pp. 1056–1073.

Vasudeva, G., and J. Anand. June 2011. "Unpacking Absorptive Capacity: A Study of Knowledge Utilization from Alliance Portfolios." *Academy of Management Journal* 54, no. 3, pp. 611–623.

Wang, N. 2007. "Measuring Transaction Costs: Diverging Approaches. Contending Practices." *Division of Labour & Transaction Costs* 2, no. 2, pp. 111–146.

Wassmer, U., and P. Dussauge. 2011. "Value Creation in Alliance Portfolios: The Benefits and Costs of Network Resource Inter-Dependencies." *European Management Review* 8, no. 1, pp. 47–64.

Weiss, J., S. Keen, and S. Kilman. 2006. "Managing Alliances for Business Results: Lessons Learnt from Leading Companies." *Vantage Partners,* https://conservationgateway.org/   ConservationPlanning/partnering/cpc/ Documents/Managing_Alliances_for_Business_Results.pdf

Whittmann, M.C. 2007. "Strategic Alliances: What can We Learn When they Fail?" *Journal of Business-to-Business Marketing* 14, no. 3, pp. 1–19.

Yoshino M.Y., and U.S. Rangan. 1995. *Strategic Alliances: An Entrepreneurial Approach to Globalization.* Boston, Massachusetts: Harvard Business School Press.

Zutshi, R.K., and W.L. Tan. 2009. "Impact of Culture on Partner Selection Criteria in East Asian International Joint Ventures." *International Entrepreneurship and Management Journal* 5, no. 4, pp. 369–393.

About the Author

Dr.Meeta Dasgupta is an assistant professor in the area of strategic management at Management Development Institute, Gurugram. She has years of both industry and academic experience. Her corporate experience is in the area of IT consultancy and corporate finance with IBM Business Consulting Services and LML Ltd. At IBM, her project engagement has been in the area of implementing Oracle Financials Applications for manufacturing industries and service industries. Her doctorate in the area of Strategic Management from Management Development Institute, Gurugram, complements her graduation from Shri Ram College of Commerce, Delhi University, and postgraduation (finance) from Xavier Institute of Management, Bhubaneshwar. Her research interests are in the areas of innovation management and strategies, diffusion of innovation, knowledge management leading to innovation, corporate or business strategy, and competitiveness of firms.

She has written several cases on strategic alliances, innovation, business and competitive strategies of organizations, and entrepreneurship that are published with Richard Ivey School of Business and the Case Center. Her research articles on varied dimensions of strategic decision making and innovation have been published in peer-reviewed journals.

She has trained mid- to senior-level executives of BSES Yamuna Power Ltd., Oriental Bank of Commerce, Canara Bank, Nepal Banking Institute, National Academy of Defense Production, Indian Oil Corporation, and others.

Index